KINETIC-HOUSE-TREE-PERSON DRAWINGS (K-H-T-P)

An Interpretative Manual

Robert C. Burns
Seattle Institute of Human Development

 Routledge
Taylor & Francis Group
New York   London

Reprinted 2009 by Routledge

Routledge
Taylor & Francis Group
270 Madison Avenue
New York, NY 10016

Routledge
Taylor & Francis Group
2 Park Square
Milton Park, Abingdon
Oxon OX14 4RN

Library of Congress Cataloging-in-Publication Data

Burns, Robert C.
  Kinetic-house-tree-person drawings (K-H-T-P)

  Bibliography: p. 207
  Includes index.
  1. Kinetic-House-Tree-Person Technique.
2. House-Tree-Person Technique. I. Title.
[DNLM: 1. Art. 2. Family. 3. Projective
Techniques. 4. Psychology, Clinical WM 145 B967k]
BF698.8.K55B87 1987   616.89'075   86-26876
ISBN 0-87630-448-X

MANUFACTURED IN THE UNITED STATES OF AMERICA

18 17 16

To my teacher
Abraham H. Maslow

CONTENTS

FOREWORD

A new test suggestion from the prolific and ever creative Dr. Robert C. Burns will be welcomed by the many clinicians whose test batteries have already been enriched and enlivened by his Kinetic Family Drawing (K-F-D) test. Those who are already enthusiastic users of the House-Tree-Person (H-T-P) test, as well as that small band of psychologists enchanted by the Tree test alone, should also find this new book to be of great interest. The notion of combining house, tree, and person all in a single drawing, although practiced by a few individual clinicians, has never before been documented. When the suggestion is added to the customary instructions that in their drawings clients or patients include "some kind of action" in their response, the test in many instances really comes to life and provides a new and important dimension, as was the case with Dr. Burns's original book on the Kinetic Family Drawing.

The imaginative interpretation of drawings to help psychologist and physician understand the emotions, feelings about self, concept of one's role in life and in relation to other persons and things is becoming increasingly popular. It is now used not only with patients or persons who have emotional problems but also with patients suffering from serious medical problems. Practitioners who do find this approach helpful will undoubtedly welcome this lively book with its wealth of detail and illustration.

To me the strongest chapter in this book is the one that reflects Burns's own very special contribution to the interpretation of drawings – that is, his chapter on "Actions in Kinetic House-Tree-Person

Drawings." As in the Rorschach, and in the other kinds of kinetic drawing tests introduced by Burns, movement responses can be one of our most important clues to the richness of the individual's inner life, reflecting the accessibility to the individual of his own inner workings, and his fantasies and images. Examples of kinds of movement which one might expect to find given here are practical and useful.

In fact most of Burns's examples are extremely lively and interesting but often violent and unusual, quite clearly drawn from a highly disturbed patient population. Indeed, the author states clearly that one of his main purposes in writing this book is to demonstrate the usefulness of his new test in individual family therapy. This use of the unusual has its merits. Goethe allegedly claimed that it is in moments of aberration that Nature reveals some of her most important secrets. Thus the unusual cases described and illustrated here definitely have their importance and impact, even for other populations. It might, however, be hoped that some student or follower of Burns will carry this special study further down into the younger ages and to a supposedly more "normal" population.

The author bases the developmental levels of performance presented here on the work of Abraham Maslow. However, many who work with children would benefit by the usual developmental approach. Thus knotholes, birds' nests, squirrels hoarding nuts, and different kinds of trunks, roots, and crowns of trees, appear somewhat predictably as young children mature. Burns's approach might gain added usefulness if clear immaturities could be delineated. A knothole might thus indicate immaturity just as much as a rotten part of a person's life.

As I feel certain that Burns himself would warn, it is important for any beginning user of this technique not to expect miracles from its every use. The responses of some individuals to any projective technique, especially to any one of Burns's kinetic techniques, are often almost stupefying in the amount they tell us about the subject. But others may respond to this or to any similar technique in a disappointingly bland way. No test in itself is magic. It is important for beginners to remember this fact.

More than this, as Burns points out, "Because we have searched for pathology and the negative in projective techniques, we have found it. Perhaps if we search for normalcy and growth, we may find these also." We at Gesell have found this to be the case. We have also found that certain responses often considered pathological in the adult are quite normal at certain stages of childhood. It is partly for this reason that we would be happy to see developmental (in other than the Maslow sense) research carried out with the K-H-T-P Test, using presumably normal subjects.

This is a highly creative and inspiring book which hopefully will be read and used as an inspiration rather than as gospel. The author, one assumes, intends some of his fascinating but unusual interpretations as possibilities rather than as guarantees. One hopes that some of his interpretations will not be taken too literally.

The proposed method is in some ways, perhaps, as much of a projective test for the reader-practitioner as for his or her subject. There are many who will be stimulated by this book to immediately add this manner of testing to their own battery. Many of the author's unsubstantiated interpretations may be reacted to by others with wonder or even disbelief. Dr. Frances L. Ilg, our own former director, and a lover of the Tree test, would have been enthralled by this book. Others may respond with more reserve. The use and interpretation of K-H-T-P will most definitely be a real challenge to many practitioners.

The successful interpretation of this new test would seem to me to require a highly imaginative, creative clinician who can get along without certainties and who is not afraid to fantasize. For such an individual it will have an undoubted appeal. The K-H-T-P will make a welcome and valuable addition to the batteries of tests of all those individuals who have already had good success with the H-T-P, the Tree alone, or the K-F-D. We welcome this book to the family.

Louise Bates Ames
Chief Psychologist, Gesell Institute

PREFACE

This book is about projective drawings, mostly about drawing a house, a tree and a person. The House-Tree-Person (H-T-P) was introduced by Buck (1948) using the instructions, "I would like you to draw a house, I would like you to draw a tree, and I would like you to draw a whole person." The paper was presented horizontally for the house and vertically for the person and tree. This technique results in three separate drawings and three separate interpretations. The H-T-P is now widely used; the instructions and interpretations are essentially the same.

The Draw-A-Family (D-A-F) was introduced by Hulse (1951). Instructions were "Draw your family." These instructions usually resulted in a linear row of static, unrelating figures. Burns and Kaufman (1970) introduced the Kinetic-Family-Drawing (K-F-D). Instructions were, "Draw a picture of everyone in your family, including you, doing something, some kind of action. Try to draw a whole person, not a cartoon or stick person." The D-A-F allowed interpretation of individual, static, non-relating figures. The K-F-D yielded actions, transactions, relationships, styles and symbols, etc., not seen in the static figures of the D-A-F.

For the past 20 years I have collected H-T-P drawings by having the drawer place the house, the tree and the person on the same page (Burns and Kaufman, 1970). Using the instructions: "Draw a house, a tree and a person on this paper with some kind of action. Try to draw a whole person, not a cartoon or stick person." The 8½" × 11" paper is presented horizontally."

I would like to share the excitement and insights resulting from a whole, interacting drawing of a house, a tree and a person on the same page. The actions, the styles and the symbols are very different from those seen in the customary H-T-P.

The technique for obtaining one unified drawing may be called the Kinetic-House-Tree-Person (K-H-T-P). Each K-H-T-P tells a story. Many of the methods of analysis developed in usage of the K-F-D may be applied to the K-H-T-P.

My special thanks to my teacher Abraham Maslow. His insights, including his "need hierarchy," when modified, help to make sense of our K-H-T-P data. Maslow's open system with its scope and developmental focus yields more hypotheses than the relatively closed, unchanging, reductionistic Freudian system for so long applied to the H-T-P.

My special thanks, also, to my son Carter for his patience, dedication, love and skill in processing this book.

KINETIC-HOUSE-TREE-PERSON DRAWINGS (K-H-T-P)

An Interpretative Manual

CHAPTER 1

THE HOUSE-TREE-PERSON (H-T-P) AND THE KINETIC-HOUSE-TREE-PERSON (K-H-T-P) DRAWINGS: VISUAL METAPHORS AND CLINICAL USAGE

Perhaps the most frequent and universal metaphor for depicting human development is the tree. The tree metaphor is used in almost every religion, in myth, ritual, legends, sacred literature, art, poetry and dreams. In drawing a tree, the drawer reflects his or her individual transformation process. In creating a person, the drawer reflects the self or ego functions interacting with the tree to create a larger metaphor. The house reflects the physical aspects of the drama. Thus the interaction and relationship between the house, the tree and the person reflect a visual metaphor created by the drawer, free from the limiting world of words. However, the action and the story of the house, tree and person metaphors cannot be clearly seen when the figures are drawn on separate pieces of paper.

HISTORY OF PROJECTIVE DRAWINGS

The systematic use of drawings to understand people has a relatively recent history beginning, perhaps, in the late nineteenth century. Goodenough (1926), whose works were extended by Harris (1963), investigated normative development of human figure drawings from childhood through adolescence and related drawing maturation to intellectual development.

Buck (1948) and Buck and Hammer (1969) introduced and evaluated House-Tree-Person drawings both developmentally and projectively. Catalogs such as that by Jolles (1964) describe in great detail the characteristic of the house, tree and person. More recently, Hammer (1971) has expanded the clinical applications of projective drawings. Machover (1949) provided a detailed clinical interpretation of children's projective drawings. Koppitz's (1968) developmental projective scoring system and analysis of human figure drawings have been widely used.

Drawings of families were studied by Hulse (1951) and his technique became known as the Draw-A-Family (D-A-F). The D-A-F instructions to "draw your family" gave valuable clinical material but often resulted in "a stiff," noninteracting "portrait" of the family.

DEVELOPMENT OF THE
KINETIC FAMILY DRAWING (K-F-D) and
KINETIC SCHOOL DRAWING (K-S-D)

To address the problems of noninteraction in the "stiff" D-A-F portraits, Burns and Kaufman (1970, 1972) developed the Kinetic Family Drawing (K-F-D) technique whereby the person is asked to draw her or his family *doing something*. The introduction of action into family drawings increased the amount of information available in these drawings, both qualitatively and quantitatively.

In their recent handbook, *Kinetic Drawing System for Family and School*, Knoff and Prout (1985) note, "If surveys of psychologists using the various drawings techniques and comparative number of books and journal articles are reliable and valid indices, the K-F-D technique is by far the most used and popular. The K-F-D has significantly expanded the general depth of family drawings in this area."

Prout and Phillips (1974) investigated school children with kinetic drawings. This resulted in the Kinetic School Drawing (K-S-D) in which the child is asked to draw a picture of relevant school figures (self, teacher, peers) doing something. Recent research with the K-S-D has included both qualitative (Sarbaugh, 1982) and quantitative analysis, which have related the K-S-D to school achievement (Prout & Celmer, 1984). Knoff and Prout's *Handbook* (1985) condenses the K-F-D and

4

K-S-D approach in a Kinetic Drawing System for Family and School.

Some advantages of a Kinetic Drawing System for projective drawings have been demonstrated. The H-T-P projective drawing technique has been widely respected and used by clinicians. The pioneer work of Buck and Hammer has been mentioned.

These pioneers in the development and use of the H-T-P have given us insight and understanding. However, there are at least three factors that have limited the use and clinical value of the H-T-P.

1. The H-T-P was developed and standardized in psychiatric settings with "abnormal patients." Much of the H-T-P literature focuses upon its diagnostic use in labeling psychiatric entities such as "organics, schizophrenics, etc."
2. Instructions for the H-T-P called for placement of the house, tree and person on separate pieces of paper. No action or interaction was possible with the figures separately drawn.
3. Interpretation of the H-T-P in an essentially Freudian matrix reduces all data and symbols to fit within this matrix.

Instructions usually were, "I would like you to draw a house, I would like you to draw a tree, and I would like you to draw a whole person." The paper was presented horizontally for the house and vertically for the person and tree.

THE KINETIC-HOUSE-TREE-PERSON (K-H-T-P) DRAWING

Something may be gained from viewing the house, the tree and the person in isolation, but the dynamics revealed in seeing the H-T-P as a whole increase the value of the tool. In this book, H-T-P will refer to drawings obtained using the traditional instructions which yield three separate drawings.

In the Kinetic-House-Tree-Person (K-H-T-P), the house, the tree and the person are obtained on one piece of paper. An 8½" × 11" paper is presented horizontally.

Instructions for obtaining the K-H-T-P are: "Draw a house, a tree and a whole person on this piece of paper with some kind of action. Try to draw a whole person, not a cartoon or stick person."

The following questions are offered to demonstrate the wide range of possible experiences while analyzing a K-H-T-P.

What story does the picture tell? What is your first impression? Whom and what do you see? What is happening? How do you feel about what is happening? Is the picture warm? Cold?

Is the house a place to hide from a world perceived as hostile? Is the house broken and empty and deenergized? Is the house a portrayal of body symbols? Does the house portray success and riches? A mansion? Does the house seem a home? Does it show signs of being lived in by a family? Is it a home in which you would like to live?

Does the person appear aggressive or hostile? Is the person blank or vacant or downcast? Is the person alive? Does the person appear seductive? Does the person seem shy? Is part of the body hidden or omitted? Does the person appear important, successful? Does the person appear part of the counterculture? Is the person warm and nurturing? Is the person joyous and energized? Is it a person you would like to be?

Is the tree alive or dead? Is the tree threatening or hostile? Is the tree weak and broken? Is the tree sexualized? Is the tree continuous or segmented? Are the branches reaching upward? Flowing downward? Does the trunk taper or broaden at the top? Does the tree seem energized? Deenergized? Does the tree seem protective? Nurturing? Happy? Sad?

Is the tree balanced? Is the tree too perfect? Has the tree been cut or hurt? Does the trunk have knotholes or scars? Does the tree lean toward the house? Away from the house? Does the tree shelter the house? Shelter the person? If you were a tree, would you like to be this tree?

What do you notice about the energy areas of the picture? Is more energy (size, pressure, movement) depicted in the house? The tree? The person?

What do you notice about distances? Is the tree next to the house? Is the tree distant from the house and person? Is the person in the tree? Is the person in the house? Are the house and tree attached? What is the relative size of the house or tree or person? Is the person interacting with the tree? The house? Is the interaction positive? Negative? If there is a sun or a moon, is it over the house? The tree? The person?

What styles are present? Lining at the bottom of the page? Lining at the top? Compartmentalizing? Lining individual parts? Edging? Birds-eye view? Encapsulation?

What actions are depicted in each of the components in the drawing? Nurturing? Dependency? Hostility? Dying? Living? Supporting? Hiding?

What symbols are present? How are the actions, styles, and symbols in the K-H-T-P related to the action, styles and symbols in other kinetic drawing techniques such as the Kinetic Family Drawing (K-F-D), or the Kinetic School Drawing (K-S-D)?

SOME CLINICAL CASES SHOWING ADVANTAGES OF K-H-T-P OVER H-T-P

The K-H-T-P is useful in understanding the dynamics in many types of clinical situations, thus enhancing the healing process.

K-H-T-P DRAWING 1A: Rebecca, Age 26

Rape, Falling Fruit Syndrome

Rebecca, age 26, produced the separate H-T-P drawings and the K-H-T-P drawing. Rebecca was raped when she was 13.

What story do you get from the fragmented H-T-P? What story do you get in viewing the whole K-H-T-P? In viewing the whole, do you feel the invasion of Rebecca's life space by the man in the tree? Do you see him as the center of the tear-like falling coconuts, 13 in number, the age at which Rebecca "fell from grace"? Do you see the tree leaning toward the house? Does the house feel like a home or a sanctuary in which to hide? Do you see the heavy lining at the bottom of the paper, perhaps an attempt to stabilize the whole?

The falling fruit symbol is one seen quite frequently in our drawings, particularly in drawings by women who in their own minds have fallen from grace. The underlining at the bottom of the picture is a style reflecting a need for stability. The rape episode and the man involved have drastically disturbed Rebecca and her self-growth. Recalling the rape episode in words helped Rebecca. Capturing the man in a symbolic interference in the growth of her tree of life was an even more healing experience. If the drawings were on separate sheets as in the H-T-P, the rapist dramatically portrayed as interfering in Rebecca's tree of life would be missing.

8

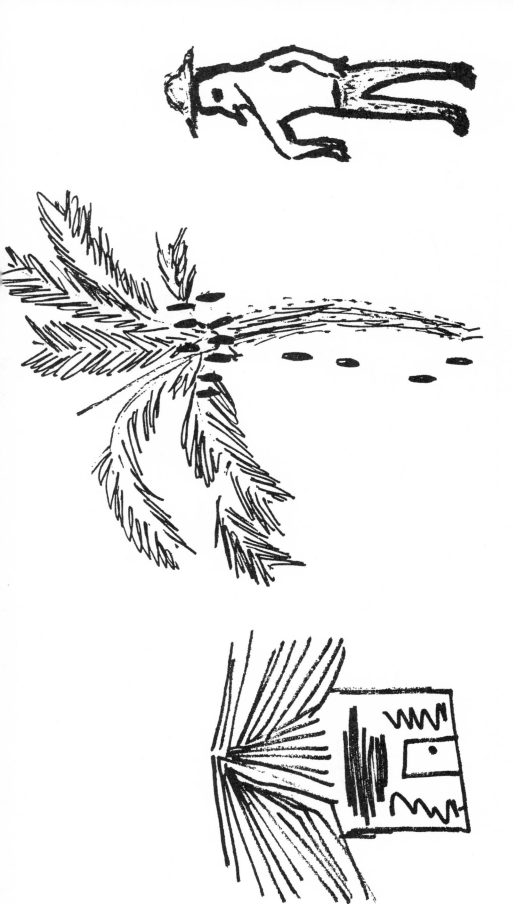

Drawing 1-P

Drawing 1-T

Drawing 1-H

Drawing 1: Rebecca's H-T-P Drawings

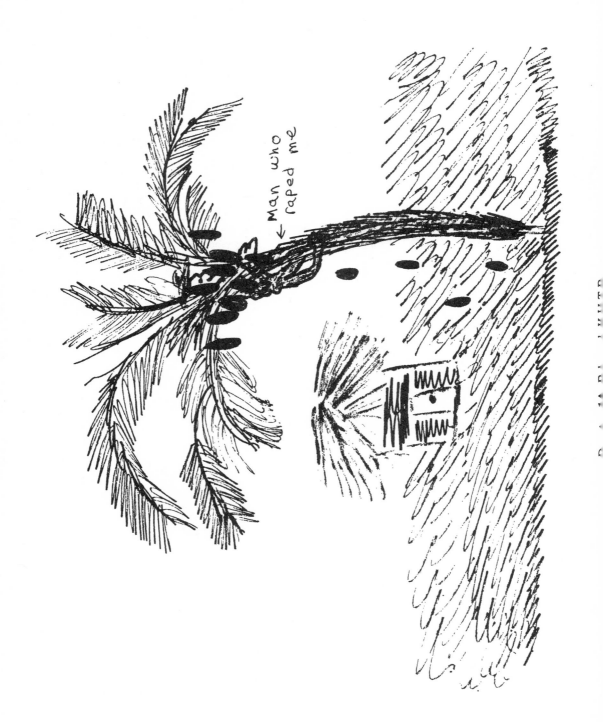

K-H-T-P DRAWING 2A: Anita, Age 64

Death Wishes Subsequent to Death of Husband

What story does K-H-T-P Drawing 2A tell? The sun shines above Jacob, Anita's husband, who died nine months ago. Jacob walks on the path leading to a home where Anita and Jacob had lived for some 40 years. The smoke from the chimney moves toward the sun beaming on Jacob. The tree (of life) has died for Anita; its trunk has narrowed so no energy can pass. The pathway on which Jacob walks has four flowers attached, perhaps symbolic of the four children.

Anita's family has sent her to many medical specialists in their search for a "cure." Anita was completely lost without her husband and frankly said she wanted to join Jacob in his sunny world. Anita was helped by transference of her attachment for Jacob to other family members. While much of her tree had died, enough of Anita's energy was rechanneled so as to allow her to survive even though still longing for Jacob.

Drawing 2-P

Drawing 2-T

Drawing 2-H

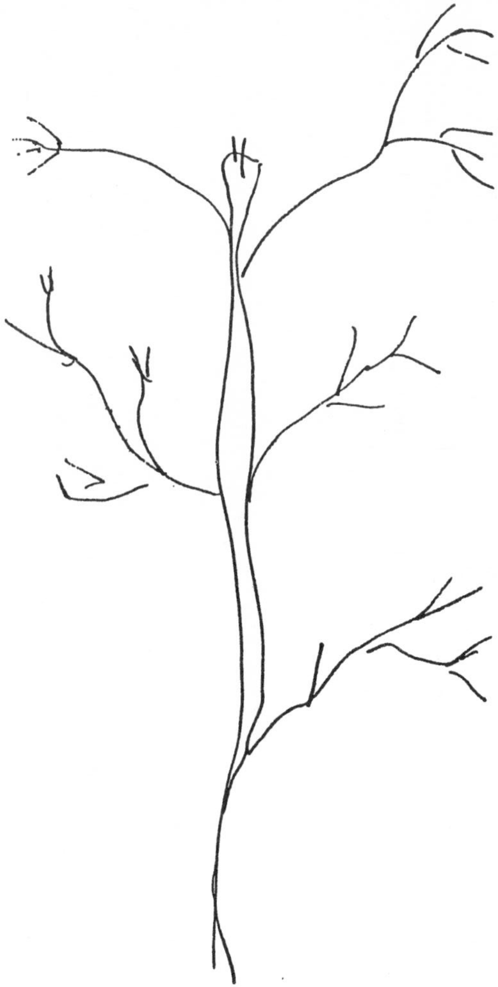

Drawing 2A: Anita's K-H-T-P

The labels within the drawing read: "Deceased Husband"

K-H-T-P DRAWING 3A: Helen, Age 28

> Chronic Depressive Reaction to Mother's Suicide

What story does K-H-T-P Drawing 3A tell? A male person is hiding in an igloo-like house. The house has no door. The tree weeps, with energy flowing downward. The trunk of the tree is narrow and ungrounded. Why all this sadness and hiding?

Helen's house, an igloo-like affair, is her place of safety. Helen's mother committed suicide when Helen was 12. The tree reflects Helen's sadness and tears associated with her mother's death. The house is a place of protection. Helen has trouble identifying with her feminine side, as suggested by the male figure in the house. The K-H-T-P helped Helen "see" her need to move forward in life. The drawing also helped Helen's husband to better understand her and to be supportive.

Drawing 3-P

Drawing 3-T

Drawing 3-H

Drawing 3: Helen's H-T-P Drawings

K-H-T-P DRAWING 4A: Peggy, Age 45

Chronic Anxiety with Mother's Attempt to Kill Her

Why is Peggy hiding in the house? Peggy has a problem, sometimes called agoraphobia (fear of the marketplace) in which she is afraid to come out without great support from those around her. The house in this case is a place for survival and protection. When Peggy was four, Peggy's mother attempted to take her own life and Peggy's. Peggy has not trusted anyone since. She is married to a man who is very supportive. Peggy needs his help to protect her from the world when she goes out of the house. Peggy prefers to be in her own territory and safe in her home. The K-H-T-P was helpful in family therapy by allowing the husband and teenage children to see mother's need for security and for them to be more supportive.

Drawing 4-P

Drawing 4-T

Drawing 4-H

Drawing 4A: Peggy's K-H-T-P

K-H-T-P DRAWING 5A: Anne, Age 53

Death Wishes Associated with Daughter's Suicide

Some eight years ago, Anne's daughter committed suicide. The
shadowy figure in the drawing is Anne's daughter. Anne says the tree
died some eight years ago. Anne is an artist and for the past several years
has specialized in drawing dead trees.

Knotholes in trees are associated with trauma and reflect a fixation
at that level of growth. The door to the home has no knob, reflecting
Anne's unwillingness to allow others to enter her "space." In her drawings, the tree is the first thing drawn. The drawer's concern with life
energy takes precedence over anything else. The heavily-shaded figure of the deceased daughter reflects Anne's anxiety in this area. Anne
once had a very flourishing life, as indicated by the outreaching tree,
but her zest for life died with the death of her daughter. Anne's drawing became a focal point for therapeutic intervention, helping Anne to
"see" and thus release attachments to the past, which she slowly did.
Her art eventually included live trees and flowers, reflecting expansion
of her own "aliveness."

Drawing 5-H

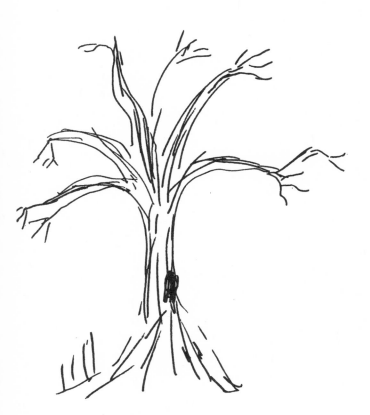

Drawing 5-T

Drawing 5-P

Drawing 5: Anne's H-T-P Drawings

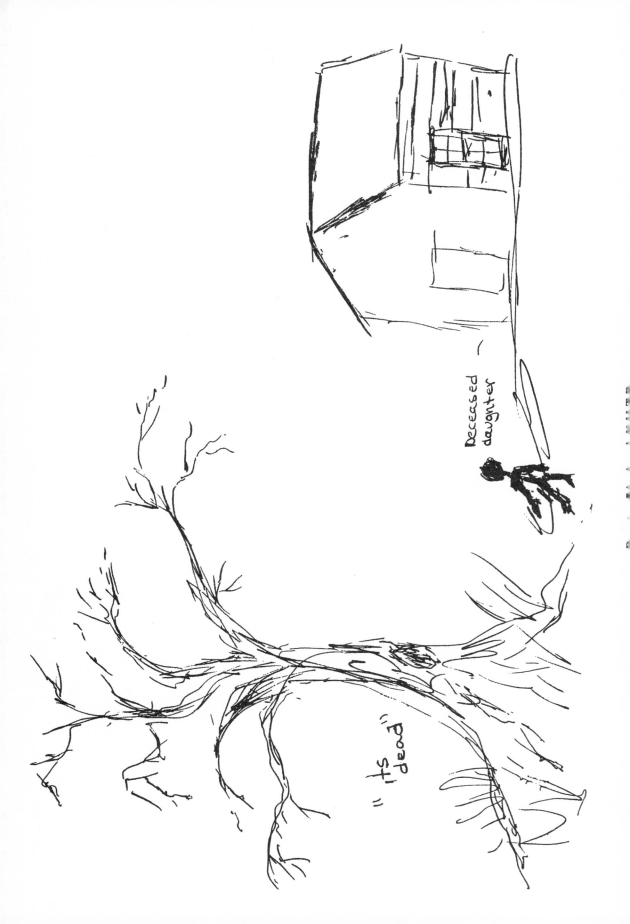

K-H-T-P DRAWING 6A: Patty, Age 29

Woman Obsessed with Success

Patty encapsulates herself in a swing. Notice how distant the house is and how the tree intervenes between the person and the house. This type of drawing is seen in people who are far away from their family and preoccupied with another branch of their life. Patty has been described as a "Yuppie." She is a young professional who is upwardly mobile and has no intention of getting married. Patty is obsessed with success in the business world.

When a tree leans toward a house, it often reflects a person drawn toward their family. When the person is on the other side of the tree, away from the home, he is usually engaged in his own pursuits. Drawings on separate pieces of paper would miss these dynamics.

Drawing 6-P

Drawing 6-T

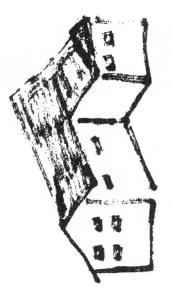

Drawing 6-H

Drawing 6A: Patty's K-H-T-P

K-H-T-P DRAWING 7A: Ron, Age 37

Burned-Out Combat Veteran

Ron is a veteran of combat in Vietnam. He returned to the States and was successful in his work, but very unsuccessful in his social life. His relationship with women was one filled with violence and guilt.

Drawing 7-T shows a dead tree with a very narrow trunk, reflective of Ron's precarious hold on life. He has a great deal of difficulty in trusting other people. The person is himself. He poignantly draws, "I love me," and is unable to trust or love others.

The house looks relatively sterile. There is no doorknob and thus the inaccessibility to his love or inner-feeling life is suggested. The drawing is all done in brown. This is typical of people who have a great need for security and earthing. It also is a common characteristic in people who have been in wars, either real ones, or in families, or in prison. Ron worked hard on "loving me," but had a precarious hold on life.

The size of the small dead tree relative to the self and the large empty brown house would be obscured if the three were drawn on separate pieces of paper. As we shall see, the positions and sizes within the K-H-T-P are important in understanding dynamics.

Drawing 7-H

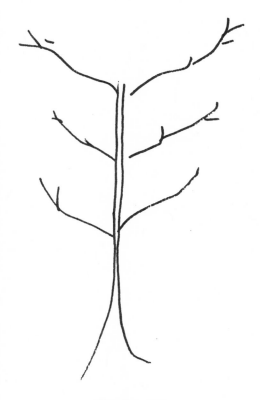

Drawing 7-T

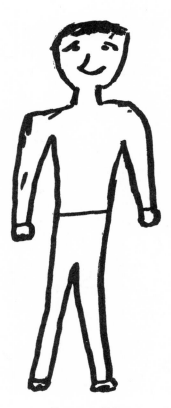

Drawing 7-P

Drawing 7: Rons's H-T-P Drawings

K-H-T-P DRAWING 8A: Mark, Age 15

Street Kid

K-H-T-P Drawing 8A was done by 15-year-old Mark. The person (self) is much larger than the house or the tree. He describes this person as "Joe Cool" and had been drawing this figure for some time. The large person in proportion to the small house suggests that Mark puts more emphasis on himself and his hedonistic tendencies than he does the security of the family. The knothole in the tree may reflect Mark's "swirling" related to his parents' divorce. The comparison of the very large person with the small house would be missing if drawn on separate pages, as would Mark's turning his back on growth and security.

Drawing 8-H

Drawing 8-T

Drawing 8-P

Drawing 8: Mark's H-T-P Drawings

Joe Cool
from 6th grade

SELF

Drawing 8A: Mark's K-H-T-P

K-H-T-P DRAWING 9A: Ed, Age 16

Street Person

Sixteen-year-old Ed drew K-H-T-P Drawing 9A. There is a similarity to Drawing 8 in that the person is much larger than the house or the tree. Ed worked primarily to "get smokes and hang out with his friends." There are 23 apples in Ed's tree. When asked about this, Ed said that when he is 23 he is going to settle down and go to school. Both he and Mark had dropped out of school and were living in the streets. Both are self-centered. Their life energy (tree) and their family (house) seem very unimportant to them at this point.

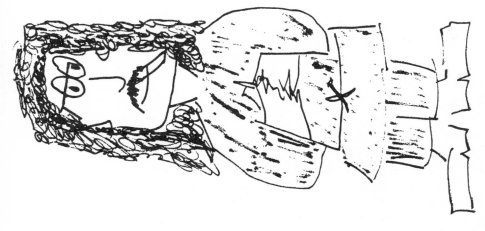

Drawing 9-P

Drawing 9-T

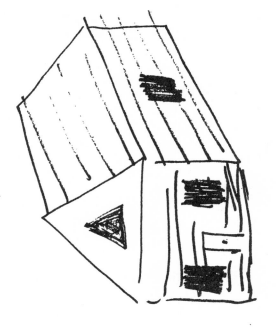

Drawing 9-H

Drawing 9: Ed's H-T-P Drawings

Drawing 9A: Ed's K-H-T-P

K-H-T-P DRAWING 10A: Steve, Age 17

Street Kid Leaving Streets

K-H-T-P Drawing 10A is by 17-year-old Steve. This drawing is somewhat different from K-H-T-P Drawings 8A and 9A in that while the person is very large, the tree has some new growth. Steve has a history of living in the streets. He wanted counseling and tried to put out some new branches of his life. The budding and rather pathetic beginnings of the tree are hopeful signs, although it would be better if the tree were moving upward rather than downward. The house has some warmth which is missing in K-H-T-P Drawings 8A and 9A. Steve expressed a desire to go live on an island in the Caribbean where "they grow pot." He had been more involved in his hedonistic world than in his own self-growth, although the tree reflects the renovation of growth and the desire to break out of his circular obsessions. Steve's tree seems to reach toward him as if to capture his attention.

Drawing 10-H

Drawing 10-T

Drawing 10-P

Drawing 10: Steve's H-T-P Drawings

Drawing 10A: Steve's K-H-T-P

K-H-T-P DRAWING 11A: Dottie, Age 27

Alcoholic Hedonist

K-H-T-P Drawing 11A is that of 27-year-old Dottie. She has a presenting problem of being a "lush." She is married and has no children. Dottie tends to run with friends who enjoy partying. She is married to a man tolerant of this partygoing. The "self" is large, with big eyes and mouth. Her hands are missing. Dottie is passive-aggressive. If her dependency needs are not met, she can become quite angry. If they are met, she becomes quite helpless, as reflected in her lack of hands. The house with the barred windows is more like a prison. Dottie felt throughout her childhood that her house was such a place and has carried this over to her present house. The tree is secondary. It seems to be much less important to her than her hedonistic self. Dottie was caught in a world of partying and having a good time, going to happy hours and not exploring her own self-growth. The relative size of the house, tree and person drawn on the same page is helpful in understanding Dottie and her priorities, which are similar to those of street kids.

Drawing 11-H

Drawing 11-T

Drawing 11-P

Drawing 11: Dottie's H-T-P Drawings

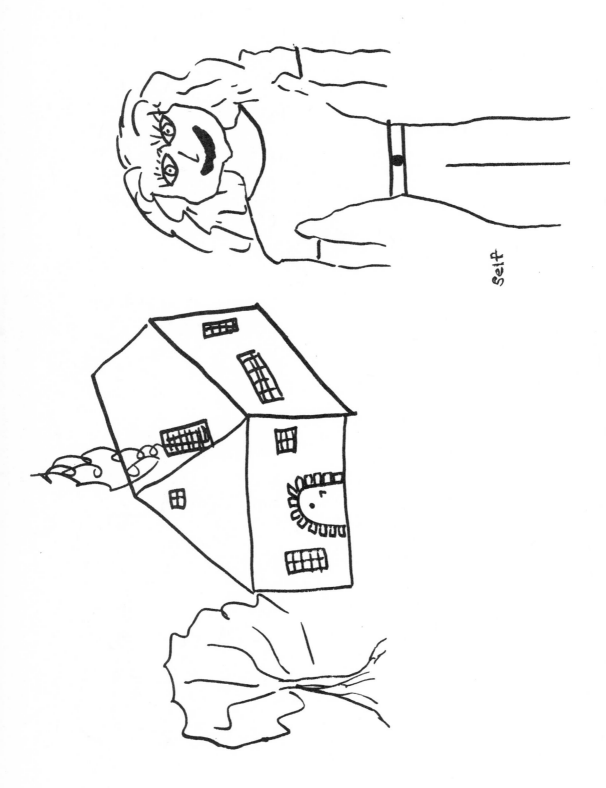

Drawing 11A: Dottie's K-H-T-P

K-H-T-P DRAWING 12A: Schuyler, Age 15

Rich Kid on Drugs Expecting to Inherit Money

K-H-T-P Drawing 12A was made by 15-year-old Schuyler who has had difficulties in school. Although brilliant, he spends his time smoking marijuana and is amotivational. The tree springs from the large house which encompasses both Schuyler and his tree.

Schuyler is to inherit a great deal of money when he is 21. He has little motivation. The house in this case probably symbolizes the power of his family.

His tree is attached to the family and he expects to be nurtured by them. Schuyler is in a passive position, as if he is watching and hoping that things will happen in his life. He seems to be indolent and unwilling to put forth effort. He is "laid back" and waits for the family to take care of him. It was necessary to move Schuyler out of the family and place him with distant "grounded" relatives who expected Schuyler to be responsible. In this new environment Schuyler gave up marijuana, did well in school, and "found himself." Seeing the tree and self nestled in the protective house (family) tells us much about Schuyler that is not apparent in the separated H-T-P.

Drawing 12-H

Drawing 12-T

Drawing 12-P

Drawing 12: Schuyler's H-T-P Drawings

Drawing 12A: Schuyler's K-H-T-P

self

Jail

K-H-T-P DRAWING 13A: Jane, Age 52

Disappointed in Life. Hopeless Feelings

Jane's separate H-T-P drawings only hint at her story, while her K-H-T-P gives more information as to why she feels hopeless. Jane's tree has no trunk and gives a feeling of instability; any wind could topple it. She is looking with unseeing eyes at an empty-appearing house which is unfinished.

Jane had a home that her husband never finished. He was a workaholic and preoccupied with his business. She had had high expectations for herself and her husband and was beginning to feel that her dreams would never come true. She had lost the will to live. In the past two years she had numerous operations and was facing more surgery. Her thoughts turned toward her family, her home and her unfulfilled dreams. Jane felt hopeless and empty inside. Her K-H-T-P was shared with her husband, Bill. He could see and understand and feel his wife's hopeless feeling. Bill cut down on his obsessive work and paid some attention to his wife and her needs. Their house was finished and Jane felt better.

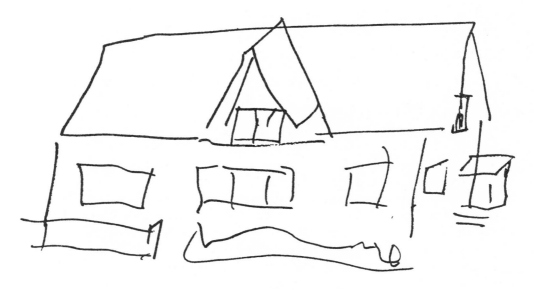

Drawing 13-H

Drawing 13-T

Drawing 13-P

Drawing 13: Jane's H-T-P Drawings

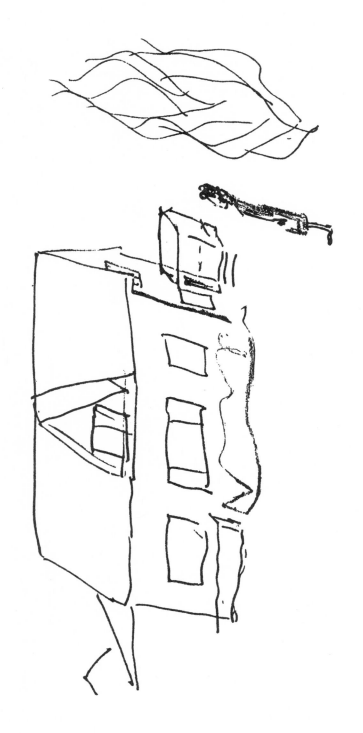

Drawing 13A: Jane's K-H-T-P

K-H-T-P DRAWING 14A: Tony, Age 29

Man Fixated upon the Past

In K-H-T-P Drawing 14A, 29-year-old Tony draws himself looking at the house in the distance, with the tree leaning toward the house. Tony has a great deal of nostalgia about the past. Tony says the house reminds him of the one he grew up in, 3,000 miles from his present home. He thinks of the past often and wishes he were back in the old home. The self is curled up on the nurturing hill, looking at the house. Tony's energies are moving toward the past rather than focused on the present or toward an upward-balanced future.

Drawing 14-H

Drawing 14-T   Drawing 14-P

Drawing 14: Tony's H-T-P Drawings

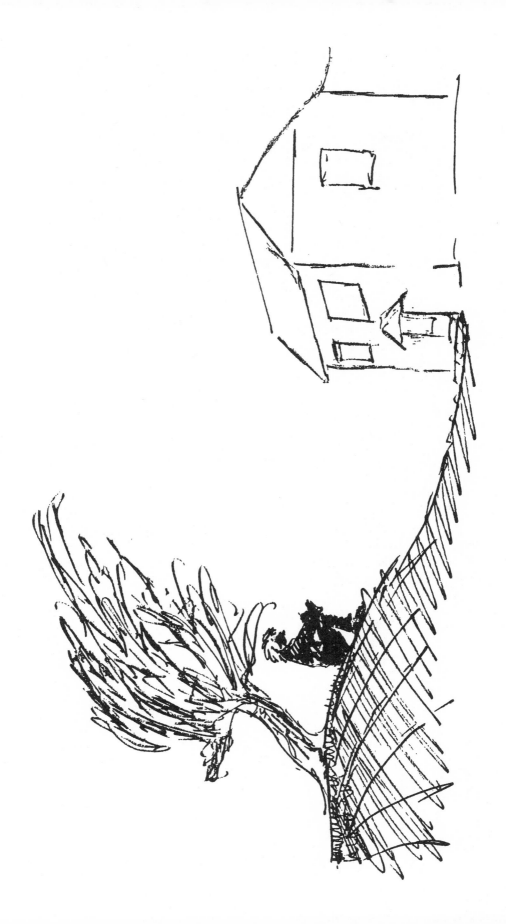

Drawing 14A: Tony's K-H-T-P

K-H-T-P Drawing 15A: Ralph, Age 28

Genius Never Grown Up

K-H-T-P Drawing 15A is by 28-year-old Ralph. Ralph was extremely successful in his musical career. He was a very creative person and put all his energy into his creative musical efforts, reflected on the right side of the tree. However, the other side of the tree where the house is located shows two tiny, long-necked figures at the window. The musician was still extremely dependent on his family. Long necks are associated with dependency. Ralph had not separated himself from his family. On the other hand, the self is kicking the tree as if obsessed with making this part of his life go. This type of drawing is found in many creative people. If we think in terms of right-brain, left-brain, his right brain is involved with his creative and intuitive process in the music world. His left brain, where the practicalities of life lie, is undeveloped and he is a small child hiding in the house.

Subsequently, Ralph looked at this drawing and started to change his life. He became balanced in terms of making a living and putting creative energies to his music. This drawing along with analysis by Ralph was extremely insightful for him in terms of having an "ah ha" experience. He did not have to change the right side of the drawing, but needed to spend an equal amount of energy on the other side, thus having a more balanced life.

In this chapter we have tried to show how the K-H-T-P gives us more and different information than the traditional non-holistic, non-kinetic H-T-P.

In the next chapter we will show how a K-H-T-P developmental approach, partially taken from Maslow's works (1954, 1962, 1964, 1965), will yield more and different information than the psychoanalytic framework traditionally applied to the H-T-P.

Drawing 15-H

Drawing 15-T

Drawing 15-P

Drawing 15: Ralph's H-T-P Drawings

SELF

Drawing 15A: Ralph's K-H-T-P

CHAPTER 2

A DEVELOPMENTAL MODEL FOR INTERPRETING THE KINETIC-HOUSE-TREE-PERSON DRAWING

Projective techniques originated in an era dominated by psychoanalytic theory. Buck who developed the H-T-P was a psychoanalyst. The interpretation of the H-T-P has largely been in the matrix of Freudian theory in a "psychopathological" population. Freudian thinking has given us insights. Like all closed systems, however, not much new enters the system. Thus, projective tests tied to closed systems have become stagnant.

Developmental systems have not been applied to projective techniques such as the K-H-T-P. Few people in psychology have looked at humans as a whole – looked at the healthy as well as the unhealthy – looked at the potential as well as the limitations. One such person was Abraham Maslow, a man with visions of our vast human potential (1954).

MASLOW'S MODIFIED MODEL APPLIED TO PROJECTIVE DRAWINGS

Maslow gave us a working developmental model defining levels of growth. As applied to projective drawings, the model includes the following levels or "need hierarchy":

Level 1: Belonging to life: Desire for life, survival, safety, root-edness.

Level 2: Belonging to body: Acceptance of body; seeking control of body addictions and potentials.

Level 3: Belonging to society: Search for status, success, respect and power.

Level 4: Belonging to self and not-self: Self now defined to include not-self as a pregnant woman accepts her child; compassion, nurturing, giving love; meta motivation.

Level 5: Belonging to all living things: Giving and accepting love; self actualization; sense of good fortune and luck; creativity; celebration of life.

Because we have searched for pathology and the negative in projective techniques, we have found it. Perhaps if we search for normalcy and growth, we may find these also.

MASLOW'S MODEL APPLIED TO K-H-T-P

Maslow's system is an open system ready to change and absorb the new. The use of closed systems has delayed progress in viewing and understanding human growth and potential.

In general, our analysis of the K-H-T-P suggests the house represents the physical aspects of our life. The tree symbolizes the life energy and direction of energy. The person symbolizes the director.

If we use a modified Maslowian developmental model, we may place each symbol at a developmental level. Because the sixth and seventh levels in Maslow's "need hierarchy" transcend our present psychological tools, we will use only five levels. Each of the first three levels may be divided into approach and avoidance (or aggressive and passive) types.

DEVELOPMENTAL LEVELS IN THE DRAWING OF THE HOUSE

Level 1: Belonging to Life

At this level the drawer is preoccupied with the question of survival on this earth or a desire to die.

Approachers: The house is a place for security and safety. A fortress or prison-like structure is common. Usually, access is limited. Doors or doorknobs are missing. The house keeps you safe from people, a sanctuary.

Avoiders: Here the person is considering leaving this earth. The house may be crumbly, decaying, old and weak. The house is vacuous and seems impermanent.

Approacher Examples:

No access

Prison-like
(barred windows)

Door too small
to enter

Charlie is a troubled man with an obsession with success. He had a violent stepfather who battered him throughout his childhood. Charlie grew up to be "macho" – determined no one would ever beat him again. He lives in a world of violence in which he is the enforcer. He is suspicious of others' motives and speaks of himself as wearing psychological armor so no one can hurt him. Unfortunately, he cannot take the armor off even with his wife and young son.

Charlie's house is a prison-fortress. His tree has a narrowing trunk. This type of trunk is seen in those who have a narrowing range of interests. They "burn out" as they get older and life "loses meaning" as they reach a pinnacle and find nothing but emptiness, as do people who climb mountains (to success) only to find that all they want was below. Charlie's person is the macho-self directing Charlie's tragic play.

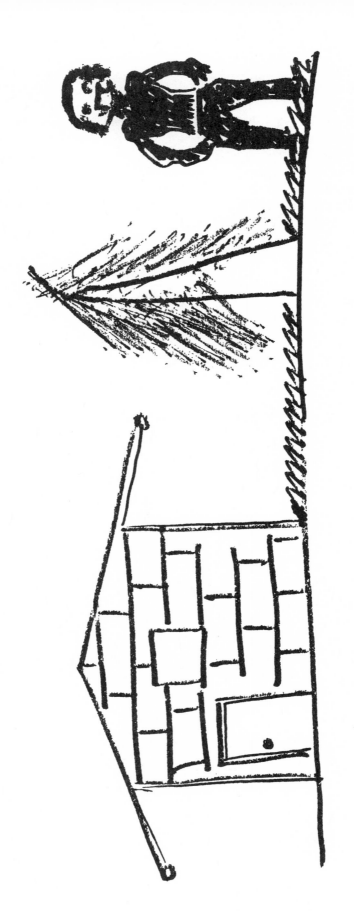

K-H-T-P Drawing 16A: Charlie's Level 1 Drawing – Approacher

K-H-T-P DRAWING 16B: Sam's Level 1 Drawing – Avoider

K-H-T-P Drawing 16B is by 40-year-old Sam. He has a history of combat in Vietnam during which he had an episode in which he was on guard duty with two others. They all fell asleep. He awoke extremely anxious and shot the other two people in a panic. He had tremendous guilt about this episode. His work is fairly successful although it has its ups and downs. He love life is extremely immature and he has had some violent episodes with a number of women.

K-H-T-P Drawing 16B: Sam's Level 1 Drawing – Avoider

The tree in this drawing looks almost like a face and has a trunk resembling feet. One suspects that the tree reflects his deep-seated guilt about the aforementioned violence. The "self" is fragmented. While the door of the house has a doorknob, it is so small that it would be difficult to enter the house. The house is sterile, with crosses on the window suggesting feelings of guilt associated with his past. The drawing is all in brown. Unlike Ron's dead tree (7-T), Sam's tree is alive and Sam was able to work through his guilt and live a fairly reasonable life without the suicidal tendencies of Charlie (Drawing 16A).

Door but no
doorknob

Impression: Place to hide or protect oneself from the enemy.
Symbols: May be barred windows. Weapons may be around.
Color: Monochromatic; brown most frequent.

Avoider Examples:

House crumbling

House vacuous

House decaying

House sagging
or falling

Impression: House is vacant or decaying. Hopeless place.
Symbols: May be moon in drawing.
Color: Monochromatic; black most frequent. Steel blue or grey next most frequent.

Level 2: Belonging to Body

The house and its openings and protrusions and walls may represent the body. Freudian symbolism is appropriate here.

Approachers: parts are emphasized. The chimney is obviously detailed, as are the doors and windows. The house may be decorated with sexual symbols, including candles, wreaths or phallic symbols. The house is sensuous and may reflect and welcome hedonism.

Avoiders: Parts may be omitted, erased or hidden. Parts may be shaded or avoided. There is a reluctance to draw the house. The house is nonsensuous. Denial is present. "X" symbol may reflect conflict areas of the body. The house may reflect a "sacred place" not to be invaded by others.

Approacher Examples:

Phallic-shaped
chimney

Candles burning
in window

Vaginal-shaped
doors, windows
rounded; wreaths

Impression: High sexualized energy. A seductive place.
Symbols: Candles, wreaths. Phallic or vaginal-shaped doors, windows.
Colors: Bright, "attractive," sensuous.

Avoider examples:

X-ing around
entrances or
extensions

Heavily shaded
roof

Heavily cross-
hatched roofs

Large number of religious
symbols (crosses) or erasures

Impression: A prim and proper house or many
ambivalences (erasures or Xs).
Symbol: Xs, religious symbols (crosses), erasures.
Colors: Avoidance of bright colors.

K-H-T-P DRAWING 17A: Betty's Level 2 Drawing – Approacher

K-H-T-P Drawing 17A is by 37-year-old Betty. At the time of the drawing, Betty was attempting to hold her marriage together. She is very dependent on her husband. This is a type of drawing where twos are repeated. We see two people in the windows, two trees and the doubling of symbols. There is a symbiotic relationship between herself and her husband. The wreath above the door suggests a female symbol of sexuality. Note the tree inside the house, suggesting her life force is dependent upon the home and husband. Betty believes "sex" will keep her marriage intact. Betty has tried very hard to keep twoness in her life and is obsessed by this. She has not found herself as an individual and is extremely preoccupied with maintaining her symbiotic "twoness." This is the type of person who might be crushed by a divorce or marry on the rebound immediately to keep her twoness intact. Betty's counseling focused upon her growth as an individual not "needing" her husband but, rather, loving him.

K-H-T-P Drawing 17B: Charleen's Level 2 Drawing – Avoider

K-H-T-P Drawing 17B is by 17-year-old Charleen. Although asked to draw a whole person, Charleen was unable to do so. Her person is desexualized. The door of the house has no doorknob and no one is invited into Charleen's space. There is no chimney and no smoke and nothing to suggest warmth in Charleen's space. The trunk of the tree is very narrow, suggesting little flowing of juices. The foliage is circular, suggesting no reaching out or direction in Charleen's energy system.

K-H-T-P Drawing 17A: Betty's Level 2 Drawing – Approacher

K-H-T-P Drawing 17B: Charleen's Level 2 Drawing – Avoider

Level 3: Belonging to Society, "Successful"

Approachers: House reflects a need for success, status, power and respect. At this level the house is stylish and expensive-appearing. If landscaping is done, it appears formal and/or polished.

Avoiders: The house is anti-successful. House does not look expensive or stylish. A counterculture house.

Approacher examples:

Large size: expensive looking   Big mansion

Impression: Expensive looking. House of successful person. House "demands respect." Opulent, stylish.
Symbols: Of wealth, respect.
Colors: Subdued colors or stylish.

Avoider examples:

House big but not expensive-looking. Has counterculture look.

Impression: A home for counterculture. Protest signs and symbols. May be eccentric or "laid back."
Symbols: Protest signs or symbols.
Colors: Eccentric, nonstylish.

K-H-T-P DRAWING 18A: David's Level 3 Drawing – Approacher

K-H-T-P Drawing 18A is by 11-year-old David. The person and the tree are relatively obscured by the large house. In this case, David is in a home where physical things are greatly emphasized. The parents are both workaholics and work in the world of showing off and displaying their wealth to others. While David is caught up in this work, as indicated by the size of the house, we see his person on the side of the tree growing away from the house. This is a boy who is beginning to question his parents' values. His own tree of life may move away from conspicuous consumption into some other area.

K-H-T-P Drawing 18A: David's Level 3 Drawing – Approacher

K-H-T-P DRAWING 18B: Jenny's Level 3 Drawing – Avoider

K-H-T-P Drawing 18B is by 33-year-old Jenny. The person is "laid back," playing a musical instrument and seemingly oblivious to the fact her house is for sale. The house is somehow not "together" and somewhat fragmented. The knotholed tree is attached to the loosely put-together house. Jenny is part of the counterculture – she's "laid back" and puts more energy into her music than into her house or tree. She has no goals or directions, as can be seen reflected in the meandering, disconnected branch style of her tree.

K-H-T-P Drawing 18B: Jenny's Level 3 Drawing – Avoider

FOR SALE

Level 4: Belonging to Self and Not-Self

At this level, dichotomies are left behind. There are no approachers or avoiders, but a unified harmony. The house becomes home. More colors are used with a feeling of warmth and caring. The curtains are not to hide, but to warm and beautify. Flowers, shrubs, trees may be added. There is a warm nurturing quality in the picture. Entry is available with doors and doorknobs. Sometimes light shines from the house. The home becomes a place to share with others in a warm atmosphere. Toys, gardening tools and flowers appear as symbols of caring and family.

Impression: Looks and feels like a home. Warm colors. Green prominent. A nurturing place.
Symbols: Flowers, toys, gardening tools, family or family things. Light or warmth may be coming from home. Pets.
Colors: Growing colors. Green may be prominent.

Level 5: Belonging to Self and Ever-Expanding Not-Self

The home is a creative effort exuding happiness and celebration. At this level the drawer accepts the self and the not-self. The home is warm and blends harmoniously with nature. Trees, flowers, birds, sun, mountains may be lovingly included in one celebration of life. The home will reflect a wholeness and a creative effort to establish a home for the body, the self, the other and the spirit.

70

Impression: A home harmonious with all. Indoors and outdoors flow together. Has all the qualities of Level 4 plus creative joyous touches. Atmosphere of love and magic.

K-H-T-P DRAWING 19: Laura's Level 4 Drawing

Laura, age 29, is a loving person with a son, age 6, and a husband, Stuart. Her tree reaches out horizontally to protect and shelter the house. The person is looking upward to her house. The house has light coming from the windows and greenery in the picture window. Laura is a nurturer who tends to give more than she gets. Her tree is slightly attached to the house. Laura is known by family and friends as a giver and a very loving, nurturing person.

K-H-T-P Drawing 19: Laura's Level 4 Drawing

K-H-T-P DRAWING 20: Marilyn's Level 5 Drawing

Marilyn, age 47, made K-H-T-P Drawing 20. Marilyn has combined raising five children with a successful career. She has never stopped growing. The picture is colorful and warm. The house and tree and person are all separate and complete. The person is whole and in profile, going about her business happily. The house is warm and decorated with flowers. The sun shines warmly over the house. The double door on the house suggests her closeness to her husband. The tree has a wide trunk and exudes energy moving outward and upward. Marilyn is a whole, joyous, supportive, loving person as her picture reflects.

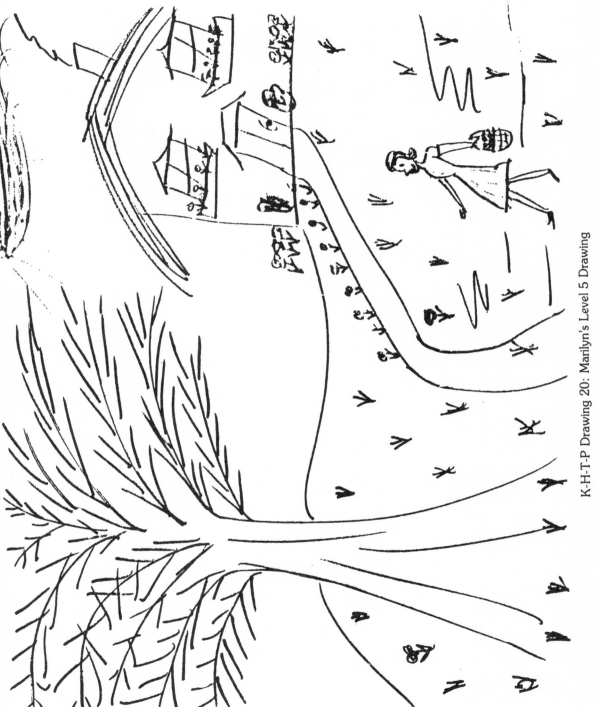

K-H-T-P Drawing 20: Marilyn's Level 5 Drawing

DEVELOPMENT LEVELS IN THE DRAWING OF THE TREE

The tree is an ancient and ubiquitous symbol of life and self-growth as portrayed in myth, ritual, legend, sacred literature, art, poetry and dream analysis.

The branching of the tree has symbolized protection, shade, nourishment, growth, regeneration and determination. The miraculous regenerating growth of the tree from seed to flowering to fruiting to seed has been seen as a metaphor for human growth and development. The tree reflects the yearning of life to grow and move from the earth to the heavens; thus it stands as one of the great universal symbols and metaphors of spirit and self-unfoldment.

The vision of a person as a tree is a uniting vision. As Jung (1979) said, "If a mandala may be described as a symbol of the self seen in cross section, then the tree would represent a profile view of the self depicted as a process of growth." Jung collected many paintings of trees by his patients.

Life force, élan vital, *prana* and *chi* are a few of the terms associated with the tree symbol. In the K-H-T-P a dead tree is associated with drawers who have lost the will to live. A stunted tree suggests a blocked growth. A narrow trunk shows a narrow range of interests and a narrow view of life. As the trunk narrows significantly, life "hangs by a thread." The age of the tree may give a hint as to drawer's developmental or energy level.

The direction of tree growth may be up and out or down and in. Knotholes in the trunk usually reflect fixations or traumas in a "swirling of the mind." An excellent summary of the tree as a symbol can be found in an article by Metzner (1981).

Level 1: Belonging to Life Acceptance of Life Force and Energy

Approachers: Tree may have talon-shaped roots or a "digging in" quality. Tree is unfriendly: may have thorns or "keep away" quality. Unclimbable.

Avoiders: Tree may be dead or dying. Trunk is narrow and foliage is absent or sparse. Tree may be twisted and stunted. The branches and foliage hang down as in the weeping willow. Branches may be broken or dead.

Approacher examples:

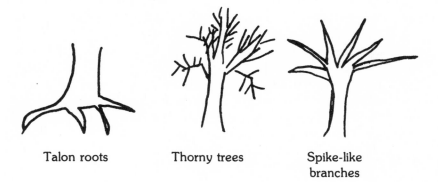

Talon roots   Thorny trees   Spike-like
branches

Impression: Unfriendly, dangerous, non-nurturing, tree formidable.
Symbols: Thorns, talon-roots.
Colors: Monochromatic.

Avoider examples:

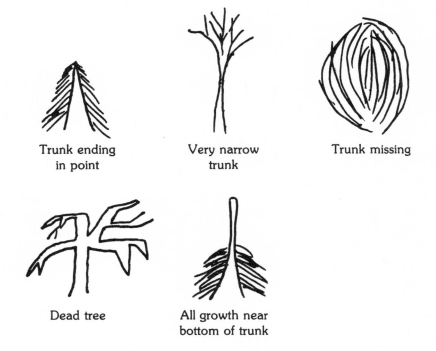

Trunk ending   Very narrow   Trunk missing
in point   trunk

Dead tree   All growth near
bottom of trunk

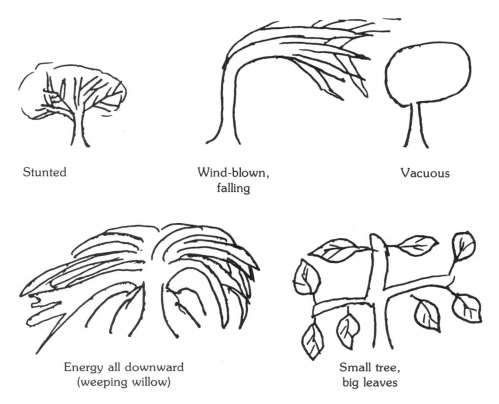

Stunted

Wind-blown,
falling

Vacuous

Energy all downward
(weeping willow)

Small tree,
big leaves

Impression: Dead, dying, deenergized or battered and empty or all energy flowing downward.
Symbols: Death, decay, emptiness.
Colors: Monochromatic.

Level 2: Belonging to Body

Approachers: Tree may have a sensual quality, may be an emphasis on texture of bark or foliage. Leaves or limbs may be phallic shaped. Sensuous colors. Tree may resemble phallus because of small branch structure in proportion to trunk.

Avoiders: Trees may have omissions or parts hidden or shaded. Non-sensuous in color.

Approacher examples:

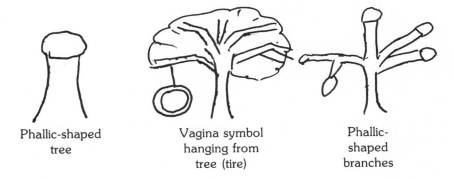

Phallic-shaped
tree

Vagina symbol
hanging from
tree (tire)

Phallic-
shaped
branches

Impression: Sexualized tree.
Symbols: Phallic-shaped tree or branches. Feminine symbols on or attached to trees (tires, etc.).
Colors: Bright, "attractive."

Avoider examples:

Xs on trunk
or branches

Rotten or
fallen fruit

Branches broken
or cut off

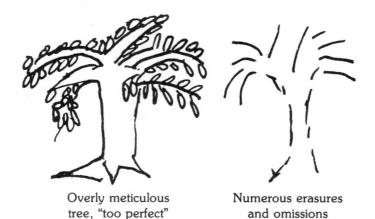

Overly meticulous
tree, "too perfect"

Numerous erasures
and omissions

Impression: Desexualized tree or proper-too-perfect tree.
Symbols: Xs, broken or cut branches. Fallen or rotten fruit.
Colors: "Colorless." Grey, brown or black.

Level 3: Belonging to Society

Approachers: Strong tree. Big, ornate, stylish. Branches reach outward
to grab and possess. Tree may be imbalanced.
Avoiders: Passive-appearing tree. Branches big but do not reach out.
Tree may be lopsided.
Approacher examples:

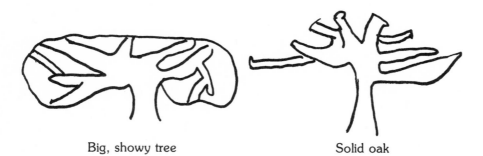

Big, showy tree

Solid oak

Impression: Big, showy, successful, powerful tree.
Symbols: Power, strength.
Colors: Power colors of the culture. Yellows, gold.

80

Avoider examples:

Big trunk,
small branch
system

Big trunk,
branches small
and turning inward

Big tree,
big leaves

Impression: Big desires and energy, but unwilling to be "successful."
Symbols: Aborted or turned-in power.
Colors: Nonstylish, eccentric.

Level 4: Belonging to Self and Not-Self, No More Approachers or Avoiders, Only Friendly Trees

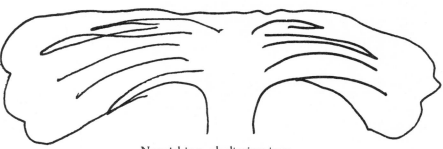

Nourishing, sheltering tree,
provides shade,
place to climb; perhaps
fruit or nuts
(no falling or fallen fruit)

Impression: Friendly tree, nourishing, protective.
Symbols: Fruit (not fallen), nuts.
Colors: Many-colored.

Level 5: Belonging to Self and Expanded Not-Self

Tree is full, whole, upward and outward-moving. Branches are continuous, not broken. Quality of vitality and celebrating, colorful. There may be birds, sun, mountains in a harmonious whole.

All the qualities of Level 4
plus upward movement, as if reaching
for heaven; harmonious; may
be mountains, birds, rivers,
flowers, other trees, animals;
uniting with all-earth and heaven

Impression: Harmonious, joyous tree blending with surroundings.
Symbols: Flowers, fruit or nuts, perhaps animals living harmoniously nearby, or birds.
Colors: Many-colored, rainbow-like.

DEVELOPMENTAL LEVELS IN THE DRAWING OF THE PERSON

The analysis of individual human figure in projective drawings is discussed in detail by Burns (1982).

Level 1: Belonging to Life

Approachers: Aggressive appearance and expression. May have paranoid features (Picasso eyes). Figure may be armed and/or formidable, suspicious.

Avoiders: Face may be vacuous or missing or very sad. People appear dead inside or furtive. Figure may be self-destructive.

Approacher examples:

| Suspicious expression | Armed or aggressive | Hurting, cutting etc. |

Impression: Suspicious, hostile, defensive.
Symbols: Weapons, uniforms (army etc.)
Colors: Drab, mostly brown; monochromatic.

Avoider examples:

No face

Vacuous, incomplete
figure

Small, frightened
figure

Anguished, tortured
expression

Impression: Hopelessness or anguish on face.
Symbols: Moon, water.
Colors: Black on grey frequent.

Level 2: Belonging to Body

Approachers: Body emphasized and sensual. Sexual characteristics often
emphasized. May be seductive. Muscles emphasized in males. Sexual features emphasized in females, including breasts, hips, etc. The
"body beautiful." People "working out," jogging, etc.
Avoiders: Body hidden or parts omitted or covered. Shame or embar-
rassment about body.

84

Approacher examples:

Emphasis on muscles,
the "body beautiful"

Emphasis on
clothes, makeup,
hair, jewelry

Seductive

Avoider examples:

Omission of body

Erasures or
omissions

Hiding body

Xs on body

Scalloped crotch

Heavy shading
below waist

Hiding body
with clothes
or weight

Making body
unattractive,
as in anorexia

Impression: Afraid of body. Ashamed or hiding body.
Symbols: Xs on body, shading of body. Omissions.
Colors: Drab. Dull.

Level 3: Belonging to Society. Search for Status, Success, Respect and Power

Approachers: Stylish. Air of success, importance. Shows status and need for respect. Conformity to power symbols in society.

Avoiders: May be counterculture. Old clothes: not success, but not weakness. Status may come from counterculture group.

Approacher examples:

Stylish, expensive-
looking

Jewelry, "I'm rich"

Impression: Proud of possessions. Successful, stylish.
Symbols: Symbols of wealth, status. May have emblems on jackets, rings.
Colors: Whatever is in style.

86

Avoider examples:

Counterculture look

Nonstylish, "poor" look

Impression: Will not conform to society's ideas of success or style.
Symbols: Counterculture symbols.
Colors: Nonstylish or conforming colors.

Level 4: Belonging to Self and Not-Self

Drawing complete and shows caring, loving, facial expression. Action is one of caring and nurturing. Compassion, reaching out, caring person.

Nurturing, caring

Helpful actions, supportive

Impression: At this level there are no approachers or avoiders. There are balanced, centered people who are nurturing to others without outer rewards.

Level 5: Belonging to Self and All Living Things

Figure reflects a celebration of life. Figure is whole, complete and often creating. Figure gives and accepts love, sense of good fortune and luck in expression. Eager expectation of the possibilities in life. Colorful.

Whole, complete people, strong but loving in expression and action. Balanced.

Impression: Whole, balanced people accepting of people, the earth and its flora and fauna and the universe. Harmony, balance. Giving and receiving.

In our next chapter we will explore variables within each K-H-T-P drawing, such as attachments, distances, order and sizes of the K-H-T-P figures.

CHAPTER 3

ATTACHMENTS, DISTANCES, ORDER AND SIZES OF FIGURES IN KINETIC-HOUSE-TREE-PERSON DRAWINGS

ATTACHMENTS

Attachments (person to house, house to tree, etc.) suggest some inability of the drawers to separate and untangle various dimensions of their lives.

People who cannot untangle their lives and who fail to have clear, unobstructed paths seem to be chronically unfulfilled and dissatisfied.

K-H-T-P DRAWING 21: Jack, Age 42

Attachments to House and Tree and Person

K-H-T-P Drawing 21 was drawn by a 42-year-old "very eligible bache-lor," Jack. Jack comes from a rich family. His father is dead. Most of the money is controlled by his mother – the death's head, ominous figure drawn in the K-H-T-P. The drawing tells a tragic tale. Jack is attached to mother and the doorless house. The scalloped tree is attached to the house. Jack has never found "himself." He has been caught in the spiderweb of the mother and the "successful" family. The only non-attached figure in the drawing is the child. Jack says he would like to start over again and untangle his tree (personal growth) from his house.

Written on all poison bottles in the Orient are two ideograms: one stands for attachment (or leaf), the other for mother. When these two ancient ideograms are placed together (attachment/mother), the ideo-gram for poison is formed (Burns & Reps, 1985).

K-H-T-P Drawing 21: Attachments to House and Tree and Person

K-H-T-P DRAWING 22: Barbara, Age 19
Attachment of Tree to House

Barbara, age 19, drew K-H-T-P Drawing 22. Barbara has not been able to untangle her own tree of life from her family's image of her. Her parents wanted Barbara to be "perfect." Barbara tried. Because of her acquired desire for perfection, nothing Barbara has done has quite satisfied her. Some four years ago she cut her wrists with a razor blade on several occasions. At 18 she had anorexia nervosa. Barbara's tree touches the heavily-roofed house and the self is low on the page and looking at the viewer, as if seeking attention. The self-figure extends off the bottom of the paper – perhaps Barbara's way to avoid drawing feet and being rooted to this tangle. Barbara finally expressed a desire to spend less time with her family and their expectations. She got on with her own tree of life without attachment to family expectations.

SELF

K-H-T-P Drawing 22: Attachment of Tree to House

K-H-T-P DRAWING 23: David, Age 46
                    Healthy Non-Attachment

David, age 46, made K-H-T-P Drawing 23. David is married with
several grown children. Despite an early guilt-producing, strict religious
upbringing, he has continued to grow, especially in the last two years.
See how the self in Drawing 23 is moving in profile – not passively
looking forward as in Drawing 22. David is looking at both his tree and
house, but is not attached to either. David and his tree of life are
growing.

SELF

K-H-T-P Drawing 23: Healthy Non-Attachment

K-H-T-P DRAWING 24: Marilyn, Age 39
        Attachment to Past, Mother's Suicide

K-H-T-P 24 is by 39-year-old Marilyn. When Marilyn was seven, she found the body of her mother who had committed suicide in a field. Marilyn has never recovered from the shock of finding her dead mother and the image and feeling of horror are still with her. She is a workaholic. Marilyn's tiny tree is attached to her big house. Notice the closed shutters on the windows and the knobless door. Marilyn is a "private person," a tormented person unable to detach her tree from the house which is so full of memories.

self

K-H-T-P Drawing 24: Attachment to Past, Mother's Suicide

K-H-T-P DRAWING 25: Beth, Age 9

Non-Attachment to Past, Striving for Independence

Marilyn's 9-year-old daughter, Beth, made K-H-T-P Drawing 25. See how Beth wrestles with the size of her tree – starting two larger trees, crossing them out, and settling for one about the size of her mother's. While Beth has some of her mother's qualities, she has some positive signs. Her tree is not attached to and "above" her house (family). Beth's person is in profile and if the drawing came to life she would walk off the page. Beth's house is not shuttered up. Beth's self-figure goes off the bottom of the page, effectively deleting her feet or her attachment to this situation. Beth will probably leave the protective world of her mother and put energy into her own tree of life.

In older couples, a passive spouse (a leaf) may be attached to an active spouse (a tree). If the tree dies, the leaf often dies shortly after of "a broken heart." Yet if the leaf dies, the tree may be "pruned" and go into a growth period. In general, attachments are blocks to growth. Mature people learn to love without poisonous attachment. We will see many forms of attachment in our K-H-T-Ps.

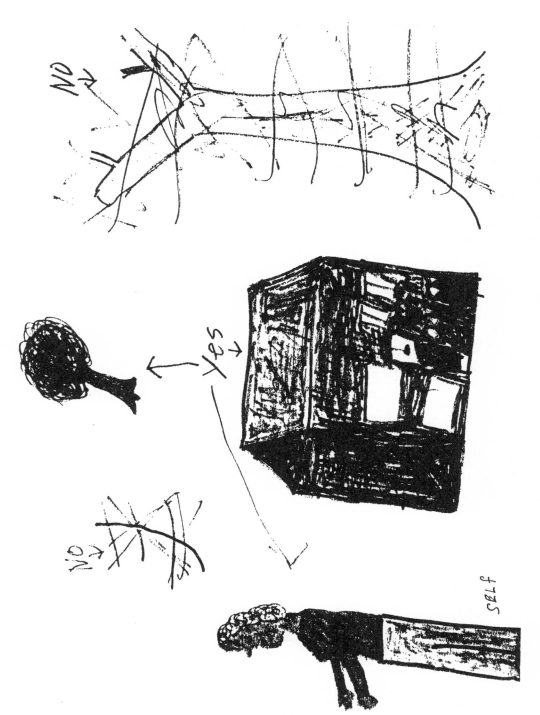

NO

Yes

NO

SELf

K-H-T-P Drawing 25: Non-Attachment to Past, Striving for Independence

SCORING FOR ATTACHMENTS

The absence or presence of attachments may be scored in the following tables:

TABLE 1: Attachments

Attachments	Present
H-T	
H-P	
P-T	
H-T-P	
None	

TABLE 2: Scoring for Figures
Other Than Self

	Present
Anti-hero	
Deceased person	
Parent	
Friend	
Hero	
Relative	
Unknown	
Other	

TABLE 3: Scoring for Additional
Figures

	Present
Anti-hero	
Child	
Deceased person	
Parent	
Friend	
Hero	
Relative	
Unknown	
Other	

ORDER OF FIGURES IN THE K-H-T-P

A few people will draw the house, the tree and the person in a row in accordance with the instructions. The great majority of drawers will impose their own order in their K-H-T-P. Here are some hypotheses as to what the order may signify.

Significance of Figure Drawn First

Possible orders are:

H-T-P
H-P-T
T-H-P
T-P-H
P-H-T
P-T-H

Tree Drawn First

Life energy and growth are most important to the drawer. This is typical of people trying to grow or stay alive. For example, suicidal persons or those losing their "will to live" will often draw the tree first. People trying to "move upward" will also draw the tree first. Of course, the tree should be viewed as part of the whole K-H-T-P if an interpretation is to have merit. Is the tree attached, dead, circular, etc.? Such information makes the "meaning" clearer.

House Drawn First

If the house is drawn first in the K-H-T-P, it may show:

1. Need to belong to the earth; a place to survive.
2. Need to belong to body. May indicate body needs or obsessions.
3. Need to belong to society; house shows success or scorn for success.
4. A home for nurturing.
5. A home for giving and receiving nurturing; a creative joyful place.

Person Drawn First

Drawing the person first suggests:

1. Concern with control of feelings of belonging to earth.
2. Showing off or hiding body.
3. Showing "success" or scorn for "success."
4. A nurturing person.
5. A giving and receiving joyful person.
6. If other than the self is drawn, it may reflect an obsession with a particular person, i.e., a dead family member, a loved one, a hated one, a hero or an anti-hero.

Our next three chapters will portray and discuss some of the actions, styles and symbols in K-H-T-P drawings.

CHAPTER 4

ACTIONS IN KINETIC-
HOUSE-TREE-PERSON DRAWINGS

Attachments as dicussed in our previous chapter are a form of action. One can sense a flow of energy along the lines of attachment in drawings such as K-H-T-P Drawing 21. The flow of energy from mother to son, from son to house and from house to tree can be "felt." Some K-H-T-P actions can be seen as well as felt.

ACTIONS WITH HOUSE DRAWINGS

In our K-H-T-P drawings, the house is the one figure that is not alive. Thus, there are fewer actions associated with the house figure.

A house may be crumbling or leaning or show other signs of deteriorating. A house stretched out horizontally may reflect the drawer's need for stability or groundedness. A house stretched vertically may reflect the drawer's need for power or perhaps for fantasy.

The tree and the person are alive and therefore give us a chance to explore actions.

ACTIONS WITH TREE DRAWINGS

1. Animal in Tree

Squirrels are most frequently in the tree, often engaged in "hoarding" behavior. They are drawn by those concerned with security. Other animals in the tree are rare and usually have some special significance.

K-H-T-P Drawing 26 is by nine-year-old Tom. Tom drew a tree in which there is a house. Within the house there is a rat on a revolving wheel. The mother says she has had recent dreams in which she feels like a rat trapped in the cage of her marriage. She has never discussed the dreams with her son. The K-H-T-P seems to reflect Tom's intuitive sensitivity to the mother's trapped feeling. Tom's branches are growing away from the house. There appears to be an escape exit from the house on the right. Tom sensed the mother would leave this marriage, which indeed she did four months after Tom's drawing.

Any animal or bird added to the K-H-T-P suggests some identification with that creature. Tom felt, as did the mother, that he was trapped and wanted to escape, like the rat.

K-H-T-P Drawing 26: Animal in Tree

2. Birds in Tree

The birds are often in a nest and usually drawn by dependent persons who would enjoy being taken care of in a nest. Birds in outer limbs may be associated with desire for freedom.

K-H-T-P Drawing 27 is by 21-year-old Mary who draws two little birds in a nest. The person is described as her lover, who is an older married man who "keeps her." He is viewed as a powerful person, as indicated by his arm with the extension of the shovel. His lack of feet suggests the instability in this relationship. In essence, this young woman is living with a man twice her age and perceives him as a father figure who will make her twoness complete. She is still in the nest and we see the long arm of the tree pointing to him over the top of the house. This side of her life is an "upper." The other side of tree, with branches essentially going down, reflects her lack of success in work and self-sufficiency. Mary's dependency upon the older man and contentment in her "love nest" were paramount as she entered therapy. Therapy focused on the underdeveloped, "work" side of her tree. Mary found an adequate job and left her nest in search of her wholeness.

Bird's Nest→

LOVER

K-H-T-P Drawing 27: Birds in Tree

3. Tree Blown and Bent Toward House

A tree bending toward the house is characteristic of those yearning for security and safety of home. This is associated with regression and, sometimes, with fixation in the past.

Terry, age 27, was a professional hockey player and produced K-H-T-P 28. Two years prior to the drawing, he was shot in an altercation. Terry recovered physically but not mentally. His once mighty tree was blown toward the house. The self hides in the house for protection. In real life Terry was unable to work and had to be taken care of like a small child.

SELF

K-H-T-P Drawing 28:Tree Blown and Bent Toward House

4. Branches Flowing Downward

This style is usually seen in those with energies flowing into the past toward unresolved problems. Weeping willow trees are often associated with depression and past fixations.

K-H-T-P Drawing 29 is by 13-year-old Walter. Walter is a rebel who drinks and runs with an antisocial crowd. He is a product of his mother's first marriage, which was ended by divorce. The mother has remarried, but Walter has never accepted the stepfather. The knothole in the tree is characteristic of children who have unresolved trauma from early in their lives. Walter's tree is moving downward. The house is brown. Walter is not close to the house, but rather on the other side of the tree, his long arms indicating his power. This is indeed an aggressive male who, for example, pulled knives on teachers in school, ran the streets and led a very dangerous life. The buttons suggest a certain self-sufficiency.

Buttons are often dependency symbols; when placed on the self, they usually indicate a person who takes care of himself. Walter ruminates about the past.

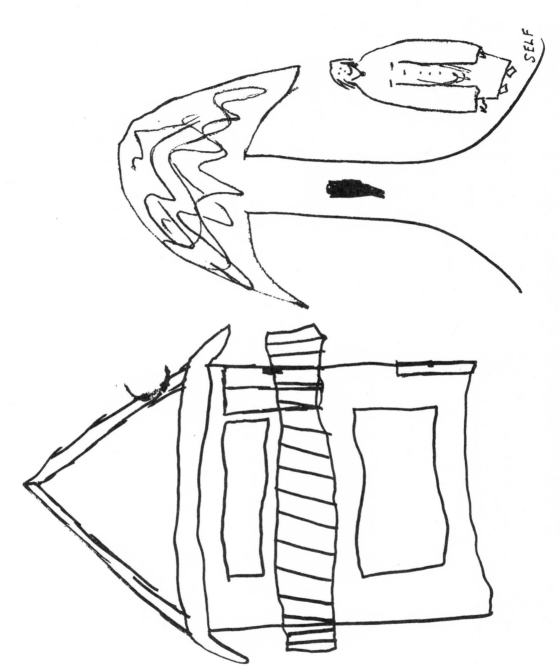

SELF

K-H-T-P Drawing 29: Branches Flowing Downward

5. Branches Flowing Upward

If the tree is well attached to earth, it is associated with upward-moving persons "getting on" with their lives.

David, age 37, made Drawing 30. He is "successful" and a nurturing person. He has many interests and "uplifting" activities. However, David puts much of his energy into bicycle racing. He works out all the time and enters races. His obsession with racing and desire for a superbody have stunted his growth. We live in a culture where energy tends to be focused on "superbodies" rather than upon balanced growth of our tree of life. Obsessive alcoholics, drug addicts, body builders, bikers and joggers often have one thing in common in their K-H-T-P drawings – the body is larger and more emphasized than their tree.

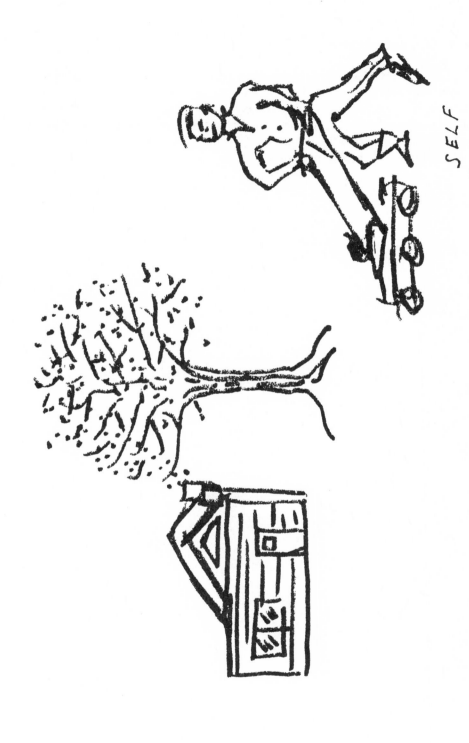

SELF

K-H-T-P Drawing 30: Branches Flowing Upward

6. Branches Reaching Outward

The sheltering tree is usually drawn by nurturing people, protective of others.

Shirley, age 45, made K-H-T-P Drawing 31. The tree reaches out in a nurturing way. Shirley is shy and dependent upon her husband. Unfortunately for Shirley, her nurturing is all directed toward her dominant husband. He takes, but gives little in return.

Husband

K-H-T-P Drawing 31: Branches Reaching Outward

7. Branches Flowing in a Circular Way

Upper foliage is circular or has a whirlpool effect. This is a very common way to draw a tree top and suggests people fixated at a level of growth with no inclinations to move up, out or down. If circularity is extensive throughout the drawing, it may be associated with people who tend to "spin out" in its extreme form, schizophrenia.

K-H-T-P Drawing 32 by 19-year-old Greg shows a circular flow from the tree to the house. Greg dropped out of school when he was 16. He doesn't work and has "no direction." The unseeing self is atop the house. In real life, Greg's parents are divorced and he has taken over the house; the mother cannot control him. Greg's tree, house and person are all attached. The mother finally sold the home and moved across the country to escape Greg's tyranny.

SELF

K-H-T-P Drawing 32: Branches Flowing in a Circular Way

8. Branches and Foliage Profuse on House Side of Tree

Trees often look asymmetrical. When trees are growing more profusely on the side toward the house, it suggests the person is putting an excess amount of energy into one aspect of life to the neglect of balanced growth.

Betty, age 41, made K-H-T-P Drawing 33. She has had a life-threatening illness since childhood, which at the time of the drawing was in a state of remission. She is married to her high school sweetheart who takes good care of her. All of Betty's branches flow toward the house. She has never worked or had many interests outside of home and family. Betty's tree is almost completely missing on the side away from the house. Her illness has kept her from exploring her own life unattached to the house.

SELF

K-H-T-P Drawing 33: Branches and Foliage Profuse on House Side of Tree

9. Branches and Foliage Profuse on Side Away from House

This is usually associated with those putting energy into their own growth and rejecting or slighting family or other house values.

Seventeen-year-old Josh made K-H-T-P Drawing 34. The growth of the tree and the branches are moving away from the house. Josh plays the guitar and wants to go on the road with "his" group. He is moving away from his family. He places himself close to the branch of the tree in which he is pouring his energy – his musical branch.

self

K-H-T-P Drawing 34: Branches and Foliage Profuse on Side Away from House

10. Fruit Tree: Fruit Falling

In pictures that appear joyous, the fruit-laden tree is part of a bountiful H, T, and P in which the fruit may symbolize creative nurturance. However, in relatively barren pictures the fruit may represent a wish to return to a nurturing past. The number of apples on a tree may give a number related to the time of fixation: "I wish I were seven again," etc. Falling fruit is most commonly seen in drawings made by those with a conscience who have "fallen from grace" and are guilt-ridden.

Maria, age 29, produced K-H-T-P Drawing 35. Maria says that she was raped when she was 17 years old. There are 17 apples on or falling from the tree. Maria is devoutly religious and could not tell her family that she had been out that night and had been raped.

The person in the drawing is dressed in black. The house has a heavy roof and an inaccessible door. Maria is very guarded about interpersonal relationships. The heavy roof on the house is often symbolic of a heavy conscience. The shape of Maria's tree is circular, reflecting spinning thoughts and "going nowhere." Maria does well in the business world but not so well in her interpersonal relations, which includes a love life characterized by masochism. The 17 apples on the tree served as a visual symbol created by Maria, which helped her to recover repressed memories of her rape at 17 and to eventually forgive her "falling."

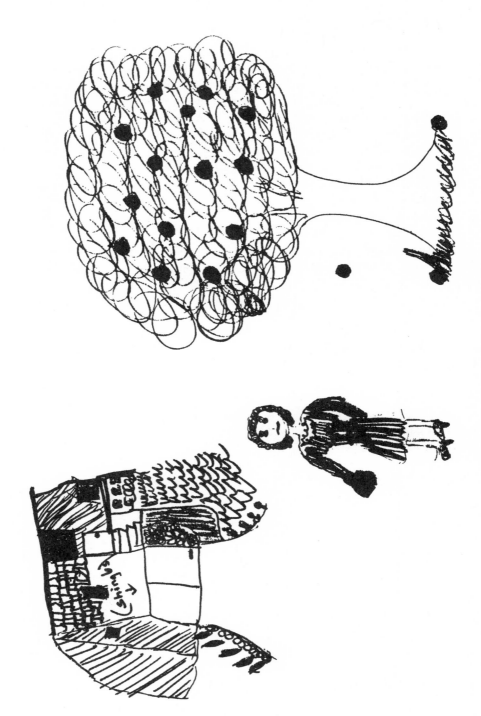

K-H-T-P Drawing 35: Fruit Tree: Fruit Falling

11. Fruit Falling, Rotting: Depression and "Rotten Feelings" Associated with "Falling from Grace"

K-H-T-P Drawing 36 was made by Mary, age 15. She was referred by a physician with a presenting problem of anorexia. She was an only child from a very religious family. Mary had been a leader in school but had suddenly given up and, according to her mother, lost a great deal of weight, changing three dress sizes in four months. Mary's tree shows fallen apples, along with one very rotten apple. Mary had "fallen from grace." The knothole in the tree seemed to reflect a "rotten" part of her life that obsessively swirled in her mind.

When Mary was in the hospital because of her anorexia, the staff would try to cheer her up by telling her how "good" she looked. These "cheering up" statements took away Mary's "victim" status and triggered loss of more weight.

Mary had tried to expel her feelings of rotteness physically, i.e., by vomiting, shedding her "rotten" body, etc. By focusing on the feelings of "being a rotten apple" and "falling from grace," Mary was able to use the K-H-T-P as one beginning experience on the road to health which she eventually achieved.

12. Tree Growing Atop House

When the tree grows from the top of the house, a significant attachment is indicated. This is seen, for example, in those who depend on the family for nurturance or are "lost" without the family, as is shown in K-H-T-P Drawing 12A (p. 43).

rotten
apple

K-H-T-P Drawing 36: Fruit Falling, Rotting

13. Person in Tree

    a) Sitting: Usually, persons trying to "get on" with their lives and trying to detach themselves from expectations or problems associated with the house (body/family/power)

K-H-T-P Drawing 37 is by 27-year-old Margo. She is divorced and has custody of her son. Margo is in graduate school working for her Ph.D. and has a great deal of ambivalence about keeping her son. We see her sitting on one limb of the tree over her son. She seems to be in the house but inaccessible, as she is in real life as she tries to get through her graduate school program. The tree leans in the direction of her son and this keeps her from completing her work. The left side of the tree, which would be away from her son and family responsibilities, is not yet developed and the tree is lopsided. She wants her son with her although there is another part of her which very much would like the son to be living with the father or with her parents. The tree is asymmetrical and Margo leans toward her maternal responsibilities. She is a recluse at this time in the academic ivory tower treehouse. Mary is trying to make a decision to either complete her academic work or get a job to take care of her son. Subsequently, Margo finished her degree while allowing her son to stay with her mother. She later remarried and kept her son with her.

    b) Swinging: The branch on which the person swings gives some hint as to where her energy is focusing. The swing suggests tension; it also suggests an encapsulation/ isolation so that the person can focus on this branch of her life.

K-H-T-P Drawing 38 is by 32-year-old Jan. Jan is a balanced woman who has numerous plans and hopes for herself. However, she has a son who is being battered by her husband, a Vietnam veteran. Her swing is on a branch directed toward the home. She is obsessed with taking care of her son and getting her family in order. Focusing on the home and being attached to one branch of her life have diminished Jan's energies in branches away from the home. The tree trunk is leaning away from the house, reflecting her efforts to balance.

K-H-T-P Drawing 37: Person in Tree – Sitting

K-H-T-P Drawing 38: Person in Tree – Swinging

ACTIONS WITH PERSON IN K-H-T-P

Actions in Kinetic Drawings have been described in some detail by Burns & Kaufman (1972). Burns (1982) and Knoff & Prout (1985).

TABLE 4: Common Actions of Person in K-H-T-P

chopping	kite flying	sleeping
cleaning	listening	smoking
climbing	looking	spraying
crawling	lying	standing
cutting	moving	sunbathing
digging	painting	sweeping
falling	planting	throwing
Gardening	taking	touching
Hanging	reclining	walking
helping	repairing	washing
hiding	running	watching
jumping	shouting	working
kicking	sitting	

The recipients of this person's actions are equally important. Here are some common K-H-T-P person actions and their recipients.

TABLE 5: Recipients of Actions by Person in K-H-T-P

Figure	Action	Recipient
person	touching	tree
person	touching	house
person	kicking	tree
person	kicking	house
person	hanging	on tree
person	swinging	on tree
person	looking at	tree
person	looking at	house
person	reclining	on tree
person	reclining	on house
person	sitting	in tree
person	sitting	in house

All of these actions with their instigators and recipients give K-H-T-P analysis a richness and scorability not found in the separately-drawn H-T-P figures.

Styles in K-F-Ds have been found in drawings obtained in many cultures (Knoff & Prout, 1985). Kinetic drawing styles have been reliably scored (Burns & Kaufman, 1972; Knoff & Prout, 1985). In our next chapter we will review some styles found in the K-H-T-P.

CHAPTER 5

STYLES IN KINETIC-
HOUSE-TREE-PERSON DRAWINGS

Styles in projective drawings were first described in detail by Burns and Kaufman (1972). These styles in kinetic drawing systems have more recently been expanded and described by Burns (1982) and Knoff and Prout (1985).

Here are some of the basic styles seen in the Kinetic-House-Tree-Person technique as well as in other Kinetic Drawing Techniques (K-F-D and K-S-D).

STYLES SEEN IN THE WHOLE K-H-T-P

1. Attachment (2 or more figures): Symbiotic relationship most frequently found where drawer has two aspects of life intertwined, usually inhibiting growth. This is similar to the style in K-F-Ds and K-S-Ds of encapsulating two figures.

2. Attachment (all three figures): Most frequently found in drawers entangled in complicated web inhibiting growth. "Life is too complicated." Need for simplification.

3. Bird's-Eye View: This is a relatively rare style for the whole K-H-T-P but may be seen in individual figures such as the person or the house. This style reflects anxiety handled by distancing and is similar to the depth responses seen in other projective techniques such as the Rorschach (Burns, 1982).

4. Compartmentalization: Characterized by the intentional separation of figures in a drawing by using one or more straight lines. Example: person in the house.
  a) People attempt to isolate and withdraw themselves (and their feelings) from others through compartmentalization (Burns, 1982; Burns & Kaufman, 1970; 1972; Reynolds, 1978);
  b) Feelings of rejection by or fear of others (Burns & Kaufman, 1970, 1972; Reynolds, 1978);
  c) Denial of or difficulty accepting significant feelings (Burns & Kaufman, 1970, 1972; Reynolds, 1978);
  d) Inability to communicate openly (Reynolds, 1978);
  e) Younger boys tend to compartmentalize less than older boys (Meyers, 1978).

5. Edging: Style characterized by having all figures drawn on two or more edges of paper (e.g., vertically, upside-down):
  a) Desire to be available or passively involved without direct interaction or involvement (Burns & Kaufman, 1972);
  b) Defensive person who stays on the periphery of issues or discussions and resists getting involved at a more intimate or deeper level (Burns & Kaufman, 1972; Reynolds, 1978).

6. Encapsulation: Exists when one or more figures (but not all) are enclosed by an object's encircling lines (e.g., a jump rope or house and/or by lines that do not stretch the length of the page):
  a) Need to isolate or remove threatening individuals (Reynolds, 1978)

7. Extension of figures above paper: Most frequent with the tree. Associated with desire for power or ascendence. Also seen in people with fantasy who dislike being "grounded."

8. Extension of figure below paper: Most frequent with person. Associated with desire to be grounded or "belong." Also seen in drawers who "hide" parts of body. Often associated with guilt or feelings of inferiority.

9. Lining and cross-hatching at the bottom of a page: Indicates a very unstable family and a yearning for stability (Burns & Kaufman, 1970, 1972).

10. Lining at the top: Lines drawn along the entire top of a drawing also include storm clouds:

    a) Presence of acute anxiety or a diffuse worry or fear (Burns & Kaufman 1972; Reynolds, 1978);

    b) Emotionally disturbed boys made more top linings than emotionally adjusted boys; supportive of Burns & Kaufman (1972) interpretations (Meyers, 1978).

11. Underlining at the bottom of the page:

    a) Characteristic of people from stressed and unstable families who need a strong foundation or sense of stability (Burns & Kaufman, 1970, 1972; Klepsch & Logie, 1982; Reynolds, 1978);

    b) Found significantly more often in emotionally disturbed vs. emotionally adjusted boys; supportive of Burns and Kaufman (1972) conclusions/interpretations (Meyers, 1978).

12. Underlining of individual figures: Lines or shading under the house. The tree or the person usually suggests an attempt to stabilize this aspect of the drawer's life.

13. Rejecting a started drawing and redrawing an entire picture: Person is threatened by the content or dynamics of first drawing and redraws a "safer" picture in the second (Burns & Kaufman, 1972).

SOME STYLES IN DRAWING OF TREES

Energy Movement: Just as in handwriting or other projective drawing techniques, people reveal styles in drawing trees as consistent as their signatures. Some general styles are very frequent.

Branches

Associated with drawers "going nowhere" in life. They do not reach in any direction but go "round and round," as does their life. A very common style.

circular movement

Associated with drawers whose energy moves into the past. Fixations, traumas, "unfinished business," yearning for "the good old days" are all characteristic of people using this style.

downward movement

Associated with drawers who are nourishing, sheltering and "reaching out" for others.

horizontal movement

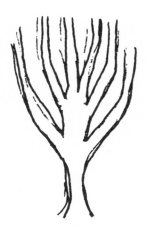

Associated with drawers who are growing and exploring possibilities for "upward movement."

upward movement

Associated with drawers who have ideas but do not complete them. "Many paths leading nowhere."

fragmented branches

Associated with drawers who have been broken or thwarted in their endeavors and feel hopeless about reaching goals.

broken branches

Associated with drawers who have a definite plan and usually finish what they start.

definite pathlike branches going
outward and upward

Trunks

narrowing to a point

Associated with "burnout." Drawers who are single-minded and single "goal-oriented." When they get to the top, they do not find what they expected and are disillusioned and depressed. Also seen in suicidal people.

expanding at top

Associated with people who become more lively as they grow older and their interests expand. Especially true if they have "pathway" branches that also expand at top.

growth at bottom

Associated with regressive people, who are often depressed and have "nothing to look forward to."

136

Associated with people who have dreams of the future and put little energy into the past or present.

small growth at top

Associated with high-energy people.

wide trunk

Associated with low-energy and often with a lack of "will to live."

narrow trunk

knotholes

Associated with trauma, often at the developmental level of the knothole. Energy spins at this level in obsessive "whirlpool" thoughts as to resolutions of the problem. Common, for example, in children's trees drawn after parents' divorce.

trunk absent

Seen in depressed, suicidal persons who have lost the will to live. Their sap has stopped flowing.

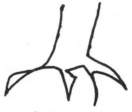

emphasis on roots

Associated with people probing into their past (roots) to help define who they are in the present.

Leaves

Associated with dependency.

large leaves

sharp leaves

Associated with non-nurturing "sharp" people.

hand-like leaves (maple)

Associated with compassionate people who "reach out and touch."

SOME STYLES IN DRAWING OF HOUSES

Doors

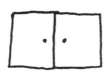

double door

Drawn by those who like doubling in the home. Frequent in adults who want a mate or to keep a mate.

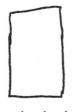

no doorknob

Associated with drawers who want privacy and do not want their space invaded.

peephole

Drawn by those who are cautious or suspicious.

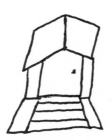

recessed or hidden

Associated with drawers who are cautious in allowing people into their space. May "test" others before trusting them.

short door

Associated with those who pretend they want people in their space but really want them out.

surrounded by Xs

Associated with those with great ambivalence about allowing anyone into their space. Especially seen in women with sexual ambivalence.

Windows

barred

Present when two or more vertical and horizontal lines are present in the window. Drawn by those who want their house to be safe or by those who perceive the house as a prison.

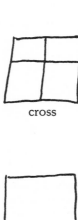

cross

Most frequent style and usually has little significance. May have religious connotation.

open

Often drawn in "empty"-appearing houses.

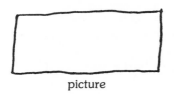

picture

Drawn by those who want to be open. An object in the picture window may be of significance as to what the drawer is showing, i.e., candles, plants, etc.

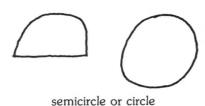

semicircle or circle

Feminine, gentle or softer people draw circular shapes.

shutters

If closed, associated with depression. Drawer works to keep sunshine out of house.

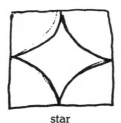

star

A style of window most frequently drawn by women. A symbol of femininity.

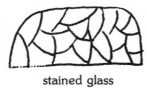

stained glass

Frequently drawn by those who feel stained or tainted. Occasionally seen by those creating an atmosphere of beauty.

In our next chapter we will explore some frequent symbols in the K-H-T-P.

CHAPTER 6

SYMBOLS IN KINETIC-HOUSE-TREE-PERSON DRAWINGS

Buck (1948), creator of the H-T-P, stressed that drawing variables may have positive as well as negative significance. He indicated how important it was to ask the drawer what was significant rather than imposing meaning from some theory or interpretation. Buck also emphasized that symbols may have idiosyncratic meanings known only to the drawer.

We have previously (Burns & Kaufman, 1972) warned against over-interpretation of drawing symbols, using as an example a picture by seven-year-old Marie (p. 145). In her K-F-D she drew a self "frightened at a snake." She drew the snake directly under her feet. Marie's problem was not sexual despite the "phallic" symbol; Marie's problem was pinworms.

Interpretation of all symbols depends on the level of consciousness of the producer of the symbol at the time the symbol was produced and the level of consciousness of the interpreter at the time of interpretation. There is obviously room for a great deal of error.

All symbols may have "meanings" at various levels depending on the frame of reference or "theoretical" bias of the interpreter. Consider Table 6. Each symbol has many "meanings."

A flower may be a sex symbol to one viewer; to another it is a symbol of magical process creating beauty.

Table 6 suggests a procedure for placing symbols at levels of need or consciousness.

Even though interpretation of symbols as "universals" or "archetypes"

TABLE 6: Interpreting Symbols at Levels Related to Maslow's Needs or Levels of Consciousness

Symbols	Need or Consciousness Level				
	1	2	3	4	5
AIR	survival breathing	aerobics jogging breathing exercises body health	power of flight, "a territory to be conquered"	nurturing life-giving	light, openness, spiritual search outward upward
BIRD	survival escape safety	food, a gourmet meal	power of eagle, "bird of prey"	dove of peace, gentleness	soaring upward free light
CAT	survival "nine lives"	sensuous, furry rippling muscles, cuddly	powerful hunter, teeth, claws	quiet, calm, serene	mystery self-contained

144

COLOR (RED)	survival "life's" blood	excitement "Santa Claus" "red flag for the bull"	fire-force, both destructive and constructive	color of warmth, nurturing, healing, energizing	part of rainbow, symbol of unification of healing energies
EARTH	survival grounded	"earthy" i.e., materialistic, pleasure seeking	power: "my territory, my land"	mother earth, nurturer	part of polarity creating energy "heaven-earth"
FIRE	survival in cold	sensual warmth	powerful for destruction construction	nurturing warmth	creative uses: steam, distilling, energizing
FLOWER	survival seeds	sensual-feminine, sexual symbol	feminine principle: overcoming through passive-receptive	beauty, love	process of natural creation of beauty and awe

(continued)

TABLE 6 (Continued)

Symbols		Need or Consciousness Level			
	1	2	3	4	5
HOUSE	place of safety, security	"house we live in," i.e., the body	symbol of success or power	place for caring, nurturing, family, a home	creative effort to reflect beauty, caring, blending with all
PHALLIC	survival of species	sensual-hedonistic	dominance, "male power symbol"	active part of creative process	creative energy actively combining with feminine energy, part of polarity of heaven and earth

146

TREE	survival, roots	body, vitality	power, size, "the mighty oak"	nurturing, sheltering, "touching"	creating new flowers, fruit, nurturing beauty, harmony
WATER	survival, embryonic stage	"juices flowing," hedonistic	"power of sea" water beats rock	nurturing, refreshing, useful	flexible, humble, serene, calm

is naive and mistake-ridden, we make some effort to understand them, especially those from our own culture. Some of the common symbols seen in the K-H-T-P are reviewed below with their possible interpretations or hypotheses.

SYMBOLS FOR WHOLE K-H-T-P

Balloons: A symbol of ascendance, need/desire for dominance or escape (Burns, 1982).

Beds: Placement of beds is relatively rare and is associated with sexual or depressive themes (Burns & Kaufman, 1972).

Bicycles: Common activity depicted by normal children (Burns & Kaufman, 1972). When overemphasized, reflects child's (usually boy's) masculine strivings (Burns & Kaufman, 1972).

Birds: Common in those seeking freedom or escape or upward growth. Bird nests are common in regressed drawers yearning for security of a nest.

Brooms: Recurrent symbol that indicates figure's emphasis on household cleanliness (Burns & Kaufman, 1972).

Butterflies: Associated with search for elusive love and beauty (Burns & Kaufman, 1972).

Buttons (oversized or elaborated): Associated with dependency or unmet needs. May be drawn on the individual looked upon for nurturance (Burns, 1982; Reynolds, 1978).

Cats: Ambivalence with mother figure (Burns & Kaufman, 1970, 1972). Preoccupation with cats is symbolic of conflict or competition in identification/interaction with mother or feminine figures (Burns & Kaufman, 1972).

Circles: Preoccupation with circular drawings or objects. Schizoid personalities (Burns & Kaufman, 1972).

148

Clouds: Anxiety is something "hanging over one's head." Number of clouds often is related to number of people in family or in a love triangle.

Clowns: Preoccupation indicative of children with significant feelings of inferiority (Burns & Kaufman, 1972). Often seen in person with history of depression or illness in family who decides to "cheer up" family.

Cribs: Indicates jealousy of (new) sibling in the family (Burns & Kaufman, 1972).

Dangerous objects: Prevalence of dangerous objects, e.g., hammers, knives, indicates anger (when directed at a person) or passive-aggressive anger (when indirectly focused on a person) (Burns, 1982; Burns & Kaufman, 1972).

Drums: Symbol of displaced anger that the child has difficulty expressing openly (Burns & Kaufman, 1972).

Flowers: Represents love of beauty and search/need for love and beauty. Drawn below the waist this indicates feminine identification (Burns & Kaufman, 1972).

Garbage: Often found in drawings of children upset over the arrival of new sibling (Burns & Kaufman, 1972). Indicates regressive and/or competitive behavior, often due to jealousy (Burns & Kaufman, 1972). It is associated with significant guilt feelings about rivalry or ambivalence toward (younger) siblings (Burns, 1982).

Figures taking out the garbage: Associated with desires to take out the unwanted and "dirty" parts (person or persons) of the family existence (Burns & Kaufman, 1972).

Heat: (e.g., suns, fires), light (e.g., light bulbs, lamps, floodlights), warmth (e.g., ironing, sunshine). Shows a preoccupation with or need for warmth and love (Burns, 1982; Burns & Kaufman, 1970, 1972).

Fire theme: Often combines anger and the need for warmth (love) (Burns & Kaufman, 1970; Reynolds, 1978).

149

Electricity: Great need for warmth, love and power which may distort or preoccupy the person's thoughts (Burns & Kaufman, 1972; Reynolds, 1978). Need for power and control (Burns & Kaufman, 1972).

Lamp: Concern with love, warmth or sexual issues (Burns & Kaufman, 1970, 1972).

Horses: Common drawing by girls (Burns & Kaufman, 1970).

Jump rope: Protection from others in the picture, from significant psychological interactions/issues (Burns & Kaufman, 1972).

Figure (other than self) jumping rope: Indications of significant rivalry or jealousy with that individual (Burns & Kaufman, 1972).

Kites (and sometimes balloons): Desire to escape from a restrictive family environment (Burns & Kaufman, 1972). A drawing of one's self flying a kite and proximity to another figure may specify the individual perceived as restrictive or punishing (Burns & Kaufman, 1972).

Ladders: Associated with tension and precarious balance. Proximity between ladder and figures may specify the focal relationship or interaction (Burns & Kaufman, 1972).

Lawnmowers (sometimes hatchets, axes, sharp instruments): In boys' drawings, the theme is symbolic of competition (usually with father) and concurrent fears of castration (Burns & Kaufman, 1970, 1972). Associated with self figure: competitive feelings, striving for dominance, attempts at control (Burns & Kaufman, 1972). Wish fulfillment towards assuming a dominant role (Burns & Kaufman, 1972). Associated with other figure: fears or feelings of threat or competition from a dominant individual (Burns & Kaufman, 1972).

Leaves: Associated with dependency; a symbol of that which clings to the source of nurturance (Burns, 1982; Burns & Kaufman, 1972).

Collecting leaves: "Collecting" warmth or nurturance or love from parents or significant others (Burns & Kaufman, 1972).

150

Burning leaves: Indicative of dependency needs not met, and the resulting anger and/or ambivalence (Burns & Kaufman, 1972).

Logs: Associated with hypermasculinity or masculine striving (Burns & Kaufman, 1972).

Moon: Associated with depression (Burns, 1982).

Motorcycles: Associated with power, dominance (Burns, 1982).

Numbers: Frequently the number of objects in the Kinetic drawing has a meaning that can be explored with the drawer. Four clouds may symbolize four anxious people in the family, a common symbol, for example, in the drawings of children with pending divorce in the family. Flowers sometimes stand for family members, etc.

Paintbrush: Often an extension of the hand, and associated with a punishing figure (Burns & Kaufman, 1972).

Rain: Associated with depressive tendencies (Burns & Kaufman, 1972).

Refrigerators: Associated with deprivation and depressive reactions to deprivation (Burns & Kaufman, 1972). Coldness of refrigerator is opposite of the light or heat symbol (Burns & Kaufman, 1972).

Shadows: These may be attached to the house, the tree or the person. The shadow suggests anxiety or "dark feelings" attached to a particular figure. This is in contrast to the "free-floating" anxiety symbolized by clouds.

Snakes: Phallic symbol indicative of sexual tension (Burns & Kaufman, 1972). It is necessary to rule out pinworms in children (Burns & Kaufman, 1972).

Snow (and other "cold" symbols): Associated with depression and suicide (Burns & Kaufman, 1972).

Stars: Associated with deprivation (physical or emotional) (Burns & Kaufman, 1972).

Stop signs (also "keep out" signs): Attempts at impulse control (Burns & Kaufman, 1972).

Stoves: Related to nurturance and oral needs (Burns & Kaufman, 1972).

Sun: Often seen in drawings of young children where it is stereotypically drawn and of little diagnostic significance (Burns & Kaufman, 1972). In older drawers, suggests need for or insistence upon warmth.

Darkened sun: Associated with depression (Burns & Kaufman, 1972).

Figures leaning toward the sun: A need for warmth and acceptance (Burns & Kaufman, 1972). Figures drawn far away from the sun, leaning away from it or faced away from it indicate feelings of rejection (Burns & Kaufman, 1972).

Trains: Symbolic of needs or perceptions of power, usually in boys, when exaggerated or accentuated in drawings (Burns & Kaufman, 1972).

Vacuum cleaners: Related to children with history of oral deprivation or unmet dependency needs; as such, an intestinal symbol (Burns & Kaufman, 1970). Symbolic of power and control: mothers using them are viewed as powerful or controlling figures (Burns & Kaufman, 1972).

Water themes (formation of water-related objects (e.g., ponds, swimming pools, oceans): Fantasy ideation (Burns & Kaufman, 1972). Associated with significant depressive tendencies (Burns & Kaufman, 1972).

Figure floating in water: Often the figure floating in the water is tied to or has significant depressive tendencies (Burns, 1982; Burns & Kaufman, 1972).

The "X" syndrome (the presence of objects in a drawing where an "X" is embedded in the object, through shading or line reinforcement, and where the object is pictorially related to someone in the drawing):

(a) Attempts/need to control strong sexual impulses (Burns & Kaufman, 1970; Reynolds, 1978);

(b) Presence of a strong conscience or superego (Burns & Kaufman, 1972);

(c) Placement of the "X" may define/identify forces and counterforces in the context of a conflict (Burns & Kaufman, 1972; Reynolds, 1978);

(d) May identify individuals toward whom the drawer feels ambivalent (Burns & Kaufman, 1972);

(e) Need to control aggressive tendencies (Burns, 1982).

In our next chapter we will explore some case studies using the K-H-T-P as an aid in understanding and helping people in their growth.

CHAPTER 7

CLINICAL USAGE OF KINETIC-HOUSE-TREE-PERSON DRAWINGS IN INDIVIDUAL AND FAMILY THERAPY: CASE STUDIES

K-H-T-P DRAWING 39: Rachael, Age 19

Bright Woman Stunted by Rivalry with Sisters

K-H-T-P Drawing 39 is by 19-year-old Rachael. Rachael is a brilliant girl but has never fulfilled her potential. She is the youngest of three sisters. The sisters are rivalrous and jealous, competing for the tiny amount of love the self-centered parents can share with them. The mother is psychologically "one of the girls." The father is a compulsive, detached scientist.

Note the hard expression on the hands-on-the-hip self-figure. The two older sisters have led "tragic" lives and seem to seek pitiful attention rather than love. Rachael has made two suicide attempts.

As we view the K-H-T-P, we see two cats (two sisters?) in the house. The cat is a frequent symbol in the K-F-D, reflecting rivalry and jealousy between "catty" people. The garbage can is also a frequently seen symbol in the K-F-D (Burns & Kaufman, 1972) related to unwanted figures in the family. For example, when a new child is born, the jealous sibling frequently draws a garbage can in hopes the unwanted rival will be placed in it along with other undesirables in the house.

Rachael's tree is beautiful but stunted. It leans toward and is attached to the house. The house looks like a prison. If the house were completed, it would be huge. The house and family with its traditions are much emphasized in this family.

Had Rachael's energies been focused on her tree of life rather than on the "catty" world of three sisters, Rachael would have found outlets for her gifts.

Rachael responded in counseling and became non-suicidal. Counseling focused on the extreme, often vicious, rivalries within the cat family. Rachael improved over a long period of time, but never achieved her potential.

K-H-T-P Drawing 39: Rachael

K-H-T-P DRAWING 40: Rob, Age 38
          Haunted Combat Veteran

    K-H-T-P Drawing 40 is by 38-year-old Rob. The moon as a symbol in drawings is frequently seen in people with depressive tendencies. Rob had been in combat in Vietnam, returned and married a woman who was very loving and had a small son. Rob became like another child to her.

    The tree was once strong but "has died." The knot in the tree has a skull-like shape. The "self" is very immature and childlike. The house has a double door, suggesting Rob's desire for twoness. With the dead tree and immature person, or self, Rob has difficulty staying away from drugs to alleviate his depressed mood. Rob's wife left him and was afraid of him. The tiny plant in the window suggests Rob's desire to "hang around" the house and be nurtured. His motivation and life force were minimal and he remained drug dependent. The moon could not warm Rob's life. The skull in his tree of life continued to haunt Rob.

SELF

K-H-T-P Drawing 40: Rob

K-H-T-P DRAWING 41: Charlene, Age 35

In Love with Two Men

K-H-T-P Drawing 41 is by 35-year-old Charlene. Charlene was divorced and at the time of the drawing was considering two men for marriage. She is a romantic who has many dreams and hopes. Her numerous trees in the picture suggest her numerous "lives" and energies. She was very successful in her work and as a family person and enjoyed people. The pathway leading to the doorway of the house suggests her desire to have people enter into her world. The top of the house has two chimneys with smoke coming out. They seem to be in the form of question marks. There was a primary question at the time of the drawing: Which of the two men would she choose? The multiple trees reflect someone who had many plans for life and many possible careers. At the time of the drawing, however, she was standing above the door, pondering as to which of the two men she would marry.

160

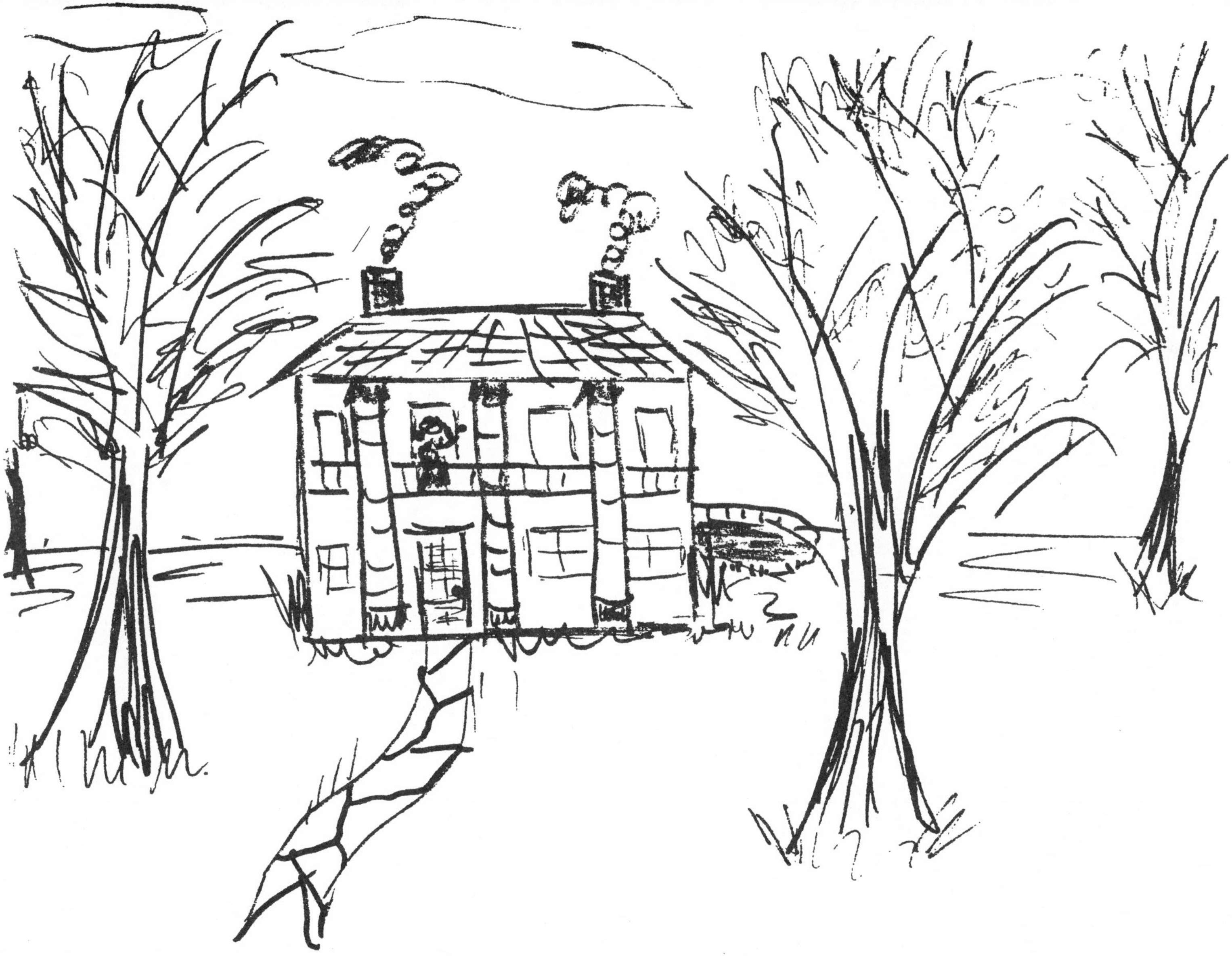

K-H-T-P Drawing 41: Charlene

K-H-T-P DRAWING 42: John, Age 38

Workaholic Seeking "Success"

K-H-T-P Drawing 42 is by 38-year-old John who describes himself as a workaholic. The numerous trees suggest his various "lives." None of them, however, have much width in their trunk. He is digging by an adjacent tree as if he is trying to get to its roots. The very large house is part of his conspicuous consumption. His wife and children on the inside are there to be protected by him. He doesn't allow his wife to work. The size of the house compared to the size of the person seems significant. John puts a great deal of emphasis on physical things. He has potential to grow but keeps going back into the past as symbolized by his digging in the roots of his tree. John's father was a "workaholic." John worked hard to understand his roots and to stop "pleasing" his father by imitating him.

162

K-H-T-P Drawing 42: John

K-H-T-P DRAWING 43: Marcy, Age 27

Fixation at Age Six

K-H-T-P Drawing 43 is by 27-year-old Marcy. She has a history of having moved from the midwest to the west coast when she was six years of age. At that time her life was quite disrupted and she has numerous feelings of looking backward and nostalgia associated with that time. She draws herself in the house. The fence around the house and the high placement of the door provide needed protection in hiding from the world the way a much younger child would do. She lives with a much older man who is a father-like figure and is primarily a protector. Marcy is fixated at age six or so and is having difficulty growing up.

In counseling, Marcy slowly removed the blocks leading to her fixation at age six. She was able to find a job but did not leave the older man.

SELF

K-H-T-P Drawing 43: Marcy

K-H-T-P DRAWING 44: Bill, Age 49

Ex-alcoholic's Dependency on Wife

K-H-T-P Drawing 44 is by 49-year-old Bill. The woman he draws is described as his wife. Bill had been an alcoholic and has been on the wagon for about six years. He is successful in his work. However, at home he depends on his wife. She is a rescuer who attempts to rescue Bill, her own children and his children by a previous marriage, who are now in their late twenties. They have a 29-year-old son living at home whom she "babies." Thus, Bill is not in charge of his own life. He has given responsibility to his wife and is very ambivalent toward her. In one way he needs her; in another he would like to get rid of her as she impedes his own growth and development. Bill worked hard in therapy to put himself in the picture and decrease his dependency on his wife.

WIFE

K-H-T-P Drawing 44: Bill

K-H-T-P DRAWING 45: Ivan, Age 55

Pruning the Past

K-H-T-P Drawing 45 is by 55-year-old Ivan. Ivan was born in a country that became communist. He rebelled as a young adult, was imprisoned for six years and then found his way to the United States. In contrast to the knotholes we see in drawings, which suggest an obsessive preoccupation, Ivan has a branch of his life that he has pruned. The pruning in this case is suggestive of cutting off part of his life that is traumatic. While Ivan has buttons on himself, they reflect constructive self-sufficiency. The tree and the house are one, which indicates Ivan's closeness to his family. He has dedicated his life to his family. Adversity has brought the family together. Unfortunately, Ivan has a chronically depressed wife and a disturbed son. He cannot detach himself from their moods and concerns. Ivan is a tower of strength, but unable to free himself from family entanglement. He has done no pruning in this stage of his life.

SELF

K-H-T-P Drawing 45: Ivan

K-H-T-P DRAWING 46: Ralph, Age 38

Eternal College Student, Burned Out

Ralph, age 38, produced K-H-T-P Drawing 46. Ralph is a Ph.D. candidate in a major university. At the time of the drawing, Ralph was working in a research setting related to his "field." He had been ready to take his qualifying Ph.D. exams for many years, but for one reason or another had postponed them.

Ralph is an only child. The family had moved to California from the midwest when Ralph was seven. Shortly after the move, the parents were divorced and Ralph lived with his mother. The parents died within a year of one another when Ralph was in his early twenties. Ralph had been married for eight years, had no children and had just been divorced at the time of the drawings. He immediately met another woman and moved in with her. Ralph's wife of eight years complained that he seemed to have less and less energy and that he seemed "burned out."

The darkened, faceless self is turned away from the house and tree. The tree has a long tapering trunk. This style of trunk is associated with people who are "single-minded" and "one-goal directed." Ralph's goal has been to obtain a Ph.D. degree – all else is set aside while this goal is achieved. People drawing this type of tree trunk seem to have less and less energy as they develop. They bore themselves to death with an increasingly narrowing range of interests. Ralph probably has double doors on the house because he "needs" another person in his life to support him in many ways. What forces shaped Ralph? What holding thoughts kept Ralph on an ever-narrowing path? Ralph's Kinetic Family Drawing (K-F-D) was useful in answering these questions.

Ralph was asked to "Draw everyone in your family, including you doing something when you were about seven. Try to draw whole people, not cartoons or stick people. Remember to make everyone doing something – some kind of action."

Ralph made Drawing 46A, depicting his family, when he was about seven. The people are dark and unseeing, as is the person in Ralph's K-H-T-P 46. The father is on a ladder (often a symbol of tension). The mother is gardening and perhaps looking down at her son.

The self has a large "A" on each side, a symbol of academic excellence frequently described in the K-F-D literature. The mother is "proud" of her son, which suggests conditional love. If the son does not make the mother "proud," then love may be withdrawn. The mother had urged her son to become a doctor so she could be proud of him. So at age

K-H-T-P Drawing 46: Ralph

38 Ralph was still single-mindedly pursuing his doctorate. Ralph had a holding thought, i.e., "If I receive my Ph.D., I'll be happy."

Ralph's K-H-T-P 46 reveals his hopelessness and burned-out feelings. Ralph's K-F-D gives us some hints as to beginnings of his ever-narrowing path.

Ralph responded well in therapy. He clearly "saw" his relationship to his family – as he said, being a dog for his father and a scholar for his mother. Ralph began a deeper relationship with an understanding, mature woman. He took up skiing, folk dancing and singing in a choir. His narrow, single-minded, "goal-oriented" self broadened. As the broadening took place, Ralph had more energy to complete one of many tasks, his Ph.D.

Drawing 46A: Ralph's K-F-D

K-H-T-P DRAWING 47: Mary Anne, Age 19

Cancerous Growth in Teenager, Hysteria

Nineteen-year-old Mary Anne was referred by a physician. She had had two cancerous growths removed in the ovarian area and was on radiation therapy. The radiologist reported some "spots" about which he was concerned. The physicians were eager to see if Mary Anne could be seen in a total treatment program.

Mary Anne produced K-H-T-P Drawing 47. The whole person is waving a greeting. The yellow house is full of life and "feels" like a home. The tree is adequate but touching the house. The picture as a whole reflects a warm and pleasant environment.

However, the door is surrounded by Xs. The X symbol has been discussed in detail in the K-F-D literature. It suggests conflict and significant attempts to control this conflict. The door in this case suggests the entrance to Mary Anne's body. The Xs reflect her sexual conflicts. Mary Anne had not had intercourse and was deeply concerned about "sex before marriage." She had a boyfriend whom she had dated for three years and she was deeply attached to him.

In the work with Mary Anne, many other projective techniques were used. One included guided imagery in drawing a shop window (Drawing 47A).

The shop window shows a mobile, a toy train set, and a Jack-in-the-box. The clown-like head of Jack is attached to a spring or a series of Xs in the area of Jack's body. Like many repressed persons, Mary Anne can draw the head of a person but denies and avoids drawing a body. However, the person in K-H-T-P Drawing 47 has a whole body, so Mary Anne under the right circumstances can overcome her repressions.

The Jack-in-the-box clown was a symbol repeated in Mary Anne's projectives. She had become a clown in her family to cheer up a depressed father. The clown role became habitual.

Using the two symbols of the Xs and the clown as beginnings, Mary Anne worked through her sexual repressions and the anger in being the eternal "happy" clown. Mary Anne became less repressed in the sexual areas and dropped the role of the eternal clown. She has been symptom-free for one year. One can, of course, have two illnesses at the same time; for example, cancer and hysteria. In Mary Anne's case, the hysteria was "cured" and the cancer abated. Whether the hysteria had any "causal" relationship to her physical symptoms no one knows. Yet it is intriguing

K-H-T-P Drawing 47: Mary Anne

to postulate that the blockage of energies in the body reflected by Xs in projective drawings might be related to body ailments.

Drawing 47A: Mary Anne – Guided Imagery Shop Window

CHAPTER 8

CONCLUSION

Each of our K-H-T-P drawings tells a story and gives a self-created visual metaphor. Verbal metaphors are created with limiting words created by others. Verbal images are but ferries carrying us to a shore of experience beyond verbal thought – a shore where one picture is worth a thousand words.

Study of the K-H-T-P allows us glimpses of this shore where things are seen more clearly.

J. N. Buck (1948) a wise psychoanalyst, combined the universality of the tree symbol with the universal human figure and its abode to form a visual metaphor condensing each individual's view of his or her life forces.

Buck's H-T-P procedure has been vitalized by the addition of a Kinetic dimension to the H-T-P forming a K-H-T-P. The K-H-T-P has been tied to the K-F-D and the K-S-D. The K-F-D gives a visual metaphor of the self in a matrix of family forces. The K-S-D gives us a visual metaphor of the self in a matrix of school forces. Combining the information from these three Kinetic drawing techniques gives us a larger visual metaphor created by the individual.

The K-F-D approach has been analyzed for computer variables in fairly extensive research (O'Brien & Patton, 1974; Burns, 1982; Knoff & Prout, 1985). This computer approach may be applied to other Kinetic drawing techniques such as the K-H-T-P.

Some say drawings are dependent on the skill of the drawer. It has been demonstrated (Burns, 1982) that 4-year-old children can depict family dynamics clearly in K-F-Ds. Thus, anyone without severe motor

177

handicaps and with a mental age of four can make a significant Kinetic drawing.

The developmental approach to analyzing projective techniques is aided by the work of humanists such as Abraham Maslow (Chiang & Maslow, 1969). The use of drawings and visual metaphors such as the mandala was explored and discussed by Jung (1979).

Both Maslow and Jung derived inspiration from Eastern systems of inner exploration such as the chakras of Kundalini Yoga. The chakra developmental system is very similar to Maslow's need hierarchy. Much of Jung's dream analysis, as well as drawing analysis, was inspired by Eastern thought (Coward, 1985).

Projective techniques remain a major Western contribution to the inner exploration of human potential. The use and understanding of projectives have been blocked by their attachment to relatively closed systems or to systems denying inner exploration. The purpose of this book has been fourfold:

1. To further develop a body of interrelated Kinetic Drawing Techniques, i.e., K-H-T-P, K-F-D and the K-S-D, into a larger visual metaphor useful in understanding individuals in the matrix of self, family and school energies;
2. To demonstrate the usefulness of the K-H-T-P in understanding humans in individual and family therapy;
3. To serve as one bridge between projective techniques and developmental psychology;
4. To serve as one bridge between projective techniques and Eastern thought.

As we broaden our view of the forces influencing the individual, other Kinetic Drawing Techniques may evolve (Knoff & Prout, 1985). For example:

1. **Kinetic Business Drawings (K-B-D):**
   Instructions: "Draw your boss, two or more employees, and yourself doing something. Try to draw whole people, not cartoons or stick people. Remember, make everyone DOING something." How would the Japanese view his work compared to an American? Are the persons drawn in a vertical or horizontal dimension? What story is told? Would you like to work here? Etc.

178

2. **Kinetic Religious Drawings (K-R-D):**
   Instructions: "Draw your (priest, rabbi, minister, guru, etc.), two or more believers and yourself doing something. Try to draw whole people, not cartoons or stick people. Remember, make everyone DOING something." What religion is viewed as most nourishing? Most frightening? Etc.
3. **Kinetic Political Drawings (K-P-D):**
   Instructions: "Draw your (president, premier, commissar, king or queen, etc.), two or more citizens, subjects, comrades, etc.) and yourself doing something. Try to draw whole people, not cartoons or stick people." What political system produces whole people? Stick people? Faceless people? What system is most nourishing? Most punishing? In which is the leader the largest? In which is the self the largest? Freest? Least anxious? Etc.

No one, to my knowledge, has done any of these studies.

Kinetic Drawing Systems including the self (K-H-T-P), family (K-F-D), school (K-S-D), business (K-B-D), religion (K-R-D) and political (K-P-D) would give us much useful information and improve our understanding of how the individual perceives his or her world. What aspects are healthy? Which pathological? How can the whole person be healed?

APPENDIX:
GENERAL AND INDIVIDUAL
CHARACTERISTICS OF THE
HOUSE-TREE-PERSON

GENERAL CHARACTERISTICS FOR
ALL DRAWING TECHNIQUES

Here are some general hypotheses regarding variables used in projective drawing techniques:

I. Pressure Factors

A. *Unusually heavy pressure* suggests:

  1. Extremely tense individuals (Buck, 1948; Hammer, 1969; Jolles, 1964; Machover, 1949).
  2. Organic conditions, possibly encephalitis or an epileptic condition (Buck, 1948; Hammer, 1971; Jolles, 1964; Machover, 1949).
  3. Assertive, forceful, ambitious persons (Alschuler & Hattwick, 1947; Machover, 1949).
  4. Aggressive and possible acting-out tendencies (Petersen, 1977).

B. *Unusually light pressure* suggests:

1. Inadequately adjusting individuals (Buck, 1948; Hammer, 1971; Jolles, 1964).
2. Hesitant, indecisive, timid, fearful, insecure individuals (Jolles, 1964; Machover, 1949).
3. Low energy levels (Alschuler & Hattwick, 1947). Depressive conditions, tendencies toward abulia (Buck, 1948; Hammer, 1971; Jolles, 1964).

II. Stroke or Line Characteristics

A. *Marked directional preferences:*

1. Horizontal movement emphasis suggests weakness, fearfulness, self-protective tendencies, or femininity (Alschuler & Hattwick, 1947; Petersen, 1977).
2. Vertical movement emphasis suggests masculine assertiveness, determination and possible hyperactivity (Alschuler & Hattwick, 1947; Petersen, 1977).
3. Curving line emphasis suggests a healthy personality, possibly suggesting distaste for the conventional (Buck, 1948; Jolles, 1964).
4. Rigid straight line emphasis suggests rigid or aggressive tendencies (Buck, 1948; Jolles, 1964).
5. Continuous changes in direction of stroke suggest low security feelings (Petersen, 1977; Wolff, 1946).

B. *Quality of strokes:*

1. Firm, unhesitating, determined quality suggests secure, persistent, ambitious persons (Petersen, 1977).
2. Vacillating direction, vague lines and interrupted strokes suggest insecurity, vacillating tendencies (Wolff, 1946).
3. Uninterrupted straight strokes have been associated with quick, decisive, assertive persons (Alschuler & Hattwick, 1947; Hammer, 1971).
4. Interrupted, curvilinear strokes suggest:
   a. Slowness; indecisive persons (Petersen, 1977).
   b. Dependent, emotional tendencies (Alschuler & Hattwick, 1947; Hammer, 1971).

    c. Femininity and submissiveness (Alschuler & Hattwick, 1947; Machover, 1949).

C. *Length of strokes:*

    1. Long strokes suggest controlled behavior, sometimes to point of inhibition (Alschuler & Hattwick, 1947; Hammer, 1971).
    2. Short discontinuous strokes suggest impulsive, excitable tendencies (Alschuler & Hattwick, 1947; Hammer, 1971).
    3. Very short, circular, sketchy strokes suggest anxiety, uncertainty, depression and timidity (Buck, 1948; Hammer, 1971; Jolles, 1964).

D. *Shading and shaded strokes* suggest anxiety (Buck, 1948; Burns & Kaufman, 1970, 1972; Hammer, 1971; Machover, 1949).

III. Size of Drawing

A. *Unusually large drawings* suggest:

    1. Aggressive tendencies (Buck, 1948; Hammer, 1969; Machover, 1949).
    2. Expansive, grandiose tendencies (Machover, 1949).
    3. Feelings of inadequacy with compensatory defenses (Buck, 1948; Hammer, 1969; Machover, 1949).
    4. Possible hyperactive, emotional, manic conditions (DiLeo, 1973; Machover, 1949).

B. *Unusually small drawings* suggest:

    1. Feelings of inferiority, ineffectiveness or inadequacy (Buck, 1948; Burns & Kaufman, 1972; Hammer, 1971).
    2. Withdrawal tendencies in restrained, timid, shy persons (Alschuler & Hattwick, 1947; Buck, 1948; Hammer, 1971).
    3. Feelings of insecurity (Alschuler & Hattwick, 1947; Buck, 1948; Burns & Kaufman, 1972).
    4. Possible depressive tendencies (Machover, 1949).
    5. Possible weak ego structure of low ego strength (Hammer, 1971; Machover, 1949).
    6. Regressive tendencies (Machover, 1949).
    7. When high on page, low energy level, lack of insight, unjustified optimism (Machover, 1949).

IV. Placement of Drawings

A. *Central placement* suggests:

    1. Normal, secure person: This is most common placement at all ages (Wolff, 1946).

    2. In absolute center of page, insecurity and rigidity, especially rigidity in interpersonal relations (Buck, 1948; Jolles, 1964; Machover, 1949).

B. *Placement high on page* suggests:

    1. High level of aspiration: striving hard for difficult goals (Buck, 1948; Jolles, 1964).

    2. Optimism, frequently unjustified (Machover, 1949).

C. *Placement low on page* suggests:

    1. Feelings of insecurity (Buck, 1948; Burns & Kaufman, 1972; Jolles, 1964).

    2. Feelings of inadequacy (Buck, 1948; Burns & Kaufman, 1972; Hammer, 1969; Jolles, 1964).

    3. Depressive tendencies, perhaps with defeatist attitudes (Buck, 1948; Hammer, 1971; Jolles, 1964; Machover, 1949).

D. *Placement on edge or bottom of paper* suggests:

    1. Need for support associated with feelings of insecurity and low self-assurance (Buck, 1948; Burns & Kaufman, 1972; Hammer, 1971; Jolles, 1964).

    2. Dependency tendencies and a fear of independent action (Hammer, 1971).

    3. Tendency to avoid new experiences or to remain absorbed in fantasy (Jolles, 1964).

DRAWINGS OF HOUSES— INDIVIDUAL CHARACTERISTICS

I. Chimney

A. *Emphasis through reinforcement or size* suggests:

1. Overconcern with psychological warmth at home (Buck, 1948; Jolles, 1964).
2. Sexual concern about masculinity (Buck, 1948; Hammer, 1969; Jolles, 1964).
3. Concern about power.
4. Concern about activating creativity.

B. *Omission of chimney* suggests:

1. Possible passivity.
2. Feeling of lack of psychological warmth in home (Buck, 1948; Jolles, 1964).

II. Door

A. *Absence of door* suggests psychological inaccessibility (Buck, 1948; Jolles, 1964).

B. *Drawn last* suggests:

1. Interpersonal contact distasteful.
2. Shyness.

C. *A very large door* suggests social accessibility.

D. *A very small door* suggests:

1. Reluctant accessibility.
2. Shyness.

E. *A side door* suggests escape.

III. Rainspouts and Gutters

A. *When emphasized and reinforced*, suggest heightened defensiveness (Buck, 1948; Jolles, 1952).

IV. Roof

A. *Significant crosshatching* suggests:

1. Strong conscience and accompanying guilt.

2. Emphasis suggests concern over control of fantasy (Jolles, 1964).

V. Shutters

A. *A closed shutter* suggests extreme withdrawal (Jolles, 1964).

VI. Rooms

A. *In general, rooms may be emphasized or deemphasized by:*

    1. Drawer's identification with a particular room.
    2. Positive or negative experiences associated with a room.
    3. Specific symbolism of room for drawer.

B. *Bathroom emphasis* suggests:

    1. Freud's "anal personality," i.e., parsimonious, petulant and pedantic. Many parsimonious people sit on the toilet for long periods, unwilling or unable to give up even their feces.
    2. Emphasis on cleanliness in obsessive-compulsive purifying rituals.
    3. A place to escape and to obtain self-mothering, i.e., long baths, etc.
    4. A hiding place. Many of those who draw overemphasized bathrooms may as children have experienced families with tension and fighting, and the bathroom became a retreat, a quiet place. As adults, they may withdraw to this sanctuary.

B. *Emphasis on bedroom* may suggest:

    1. A retreat for depressed drawers, in which case it will look quiet and gloomy.
    2. A place for sexual activity.
    3. A place for invalids.

C. *Dining room and kitchen emphasis* may suggest a place for nurturing. Orality or dependence may be a characteristic of the drawer's strong need for affection.

D. *Living room emphasis* may suggest a place for socialization.

E. *Recreation room emphasis* may suggest a place for playing.

F. *Work room emphasis* may suggest a workaholic.

G. *Rooms absent* may suggest unwillingness to draw room because of unpleasantness.

H. *Rotten or filthy* suggest a hostility towards home or towards self.

VII. Paper Siding

A. *Paper siding* may suggest generalized insecurity.

VIII. Shrubs and Flowers

A. *Shrubs or flowers* may suggest persons (Jolles, 1964).

IX. Stained Glass

A. *Stained glass* may suggest:

    1. Guilt or being "stained."
    2. Spiritual quest for beauty.

X. Steps and Walkways

A. *Steps or walkways* may suggest welcoming of social interaction. "Welcome to my space."

B. *Steps leading to blank wall* suggest conflicts regarding accessibility.

C. *Walkways well proportioned and easily drawn* suggest control and tact socially (Buck, 1948; Hammer, 1969; Jolles, 1964).

D. *Long walkways or steps leading to house* suggest guarded accessibility.

XI. Walls

A. *Strong walls* suggest a sturdy self.

B. *Thin walls* suggest:

1. A weak self.
2. Vulnerable self.

C. *Overemphasized horizontal dimension* suggests a practicality and a need for groundedness.

D. *Overemphasized vertical dimension* suggests an active fantasy life.

E. *Crumbling walls* suggest a disintegrating personality.

XII. Windows

A. *Absence of windows* suggests withdrawal and possible paranoid tendencies.

B. *Many windows* suggest openness and desire for environmental contact.

C. *Curtained windows* suggest:

1. Concern for beauty at home.
2. Reserved accessibility.

D. *Very small in size* suggests:

1. Psychological inaccessibility.
2. Shyness.

DRAWINGS OF TREES—
INDIVIDUAL CHARACTERISTICS

Animals in Trees

Relatively rare. Each animal has its own features with which the drawer may identify. Perhaps most frequent is the squirrel, often drawn by those who have a history of deprivation with subsequent hoarding behavior. Some dependent persons create a warm, protective uterine existence, placing the animal in a hole in the tree (Jolles, 1964).

Apple Tree

Apples falling or fallen indicate feelings of rejection or guilt. "Fallen angel" syndrome often seen subsequent to a trauma such as rape (Jolles, 1964).

Bark

Broken: difficult, stormy history. Heavily drawn: anxiety. Meticulously drawn: compulsiveness, rigidity, careful attempts to control obsessions (Jolles, 1964).

Branches

A. *General*

Organized, balanced, appropriately formed branches attempt to grow in a vigorous and balanced way. Degree of flexibility, size, number and balance indicates a reaching out to environment for nurturing and growth.

B. *Specific*

1. Absolute symmetry in detailed manner suggests compulsive need for control (Jolles, 1964).
2. Asymmetry toward house may indicate concerns, attachment to family, security. Away from house may indicate growing independently, moving from family attachments.
3. Broken or cut-off branches suggest feeling of trauma or castration (Hammer, 1969; Jolles, 1964).
4. Dead branches may indicate feelings of loss or emptiness in some branch of life.
5. Disconnected or broken branches may indicate a dreamer or fantasist who does not follow through in systematic, organized fashion.
6. Branches hanging downward, especially a weeping willow, indicate tending to "be sorry" and have thoughts moving into past.
7. Branches moving upward indicate reaching for opportunities in environment.

8. New growth protruding from trunk may indicate new hope or new movement toward trusting environment.
9. Branches that are overly large in relation to trunk indicate feelings of inadequacy, with excessive striving to get satisfaction from environment.
10. People swinging on branches may suggest tension in focusing on one branch of life at the expense of others.
11. A tree house on a branch may suggest attempts to find protection from a threatening environment.
12. Tiny branches on a large trunk suggest inability to get satisfaction from environment.
13. A tree upon a hill is frequently seen in maternal dependence. Occasionally it is seen in upward strivings, especially if the tree is rugged and large.
14. Large leaves suggest dependency associated with feelings of inadequacy (Burns & Kaufman, 1972; Burns, 1982; Jolles, 1964).
15. Saplings indicate immaturity and aggression (Buck, 1948).

Roots

A. *General*

Emphasis on the tree roots suggests attention to past usually associated with immaturity or "unsettled business." Persons unsure of themselves often try to find "who they are" by defining themselves in terms of past events or persons. Usually this "looking backward" diminishes growth.

1. Dead roots indicate obsessive-depressive feelings of early life (Jolles, 1964).
2. Talon-like roots suggest persons or places held on to.
3. Roots of the edge of the paper indicate insecurity feelings. Need for stability.

Trunks

A. *General*

Tree trunks are said to reflect feelings of energy, élan vital, libido, life force in growth and development. Traumatic indices on the trunk seem to reflect the age a severe trauma was experienced. Trunks diminishing at the top suggest a diminishing vitality, a "burning out."

B. *Specific*

1. Deep shading on a trunk suggests pervasive anxieties.
2. A faintly-drawn trunk suggests passivity.
3. Scars on the trunk may reflect traumatic experiences (Buck, 1948; Jolles, 1964).
4. Slender or very narrow trunks indicate precarious adjustment and precarious hold on life.
5. Windblown trunks suggest pressures and tensions from environment.

DRAWINGS OF PERSONS— INDIVIDUAL CHARACTERISTICS

Head

A. *Unusually large heads* suggest:

1. Overvaluation of intelligence or high intellectual aspiration (Buck, 1948).
2. Dissatisfaction with one's physique (Buck, 1948).
3. Possible organicity or preoccupation with headaches (DiLeo, 1973).
4. Possible subnormal intelligence (Machover, 1949).
5. Children normally draw proportionately larger heads than adults (Machover, 1949).

B. *Unusually small heads* suggest:

1. Feelings of inadequacy or impotency – intellectually, socially or sexually (DiLeo, 1973; Jolles, 1964; Machover, 1949).
2. Feelings of inferiority or weakness (Burns & Kaufman, 1972; Machover, 1949).

Hair

A. *Hair emphasis on head, chest, beard or elsewhere* suggests:

1. Virility striving; sexual preoccupation (Buck, 1948; Jolles, 1964; Machover, 1949).

2. Probable narcissism expressed by elaborate coiffures, exceptionally wavy and glamorous hair, usually with other cosmetic emphasis. Possible psychosomatic or asthmatic condition, or narcissism as in adolescent females, perhaps with inclination toward sexual delinquency (Buck, 1948; Machover, 1949).

B. *Hair omitted or inadequate* suggests low physical vigor (Machover, 1949).

Facial Features

A. *Omission of facial features with rest adequately drawn* suggests:
   1. Evasiveness and superficiality in interpersonal relationships (Burns & Kaufman, 1972; Machover, 1949).
   2. Inadequate environmental contact (Machover, 1949).
   3. Poor prognosis in therapy; satisfactory drawings of features suggest favorable prognosis (Machover, 1949).

B. *Dim facial features* suggest:
   1. Withdrawal tendencies, especially when in profile (Machover, 1949).
   2. Timidity and self-consciousness in interpersonal relations (Burns & Kaufman, 1972; Machover, 1949).

C. *Overemphasis and strong reinforcement of facial features* suggest:
   1. Feelings of inadequacy and weakness compensated by aggressive and socially dominant behavior (Machover, 1949).

Eyes and Eyebrows

A. *Unusually large eyes* suggest:
   1. Suspiciousness, ideas of reference, or other paranoid characteristics, perhaps with aggressive acting-out tendencies, especially if eyes are dark, menacing or piercing (DiLeo, 1973; Machover, 1949).
   2. Possible anxiety, especially if shaded (Machover, 1949).
   3. Hypersensitivity to social opinion (Machover, 1949).
   4. Extraversive, socially outgoing tendencies (Machover, 1949).

192

5. Females normally make larger and more detailed eyes than males (Machover, 1949).

B. *Unusually small or closed eyes* suggest:

1. Introversive tendencies (Machover, 1949).
2. Self-absorption; contemplative, introspective tendencies (Machover, 1949).
3. Large orbit of eye with tiny eye suggests strong visual curiosity and guilt feelings, probably regarding voyeuristic conflicts (Machover, 1949).
4. Pupils omitted, so-called "Empty Eye," suggests an introversive, self-absorbed tendency in persons who are not interested in perceiving their environment and who perceive it only as vague and undifferentiated (Burns & Kaufman, 1972; Machover, 1949).
5. "Picasso" eye (single eye drawn disoriented on or in the middle of a figure's face) indicates excessive concern and/or vigilance in relation to another figure or significant other (Burns & Kaufman, 1972).

C. *Eyebrows and Eyelashes*:

1. Considerable elaboration, especially with very trim eyebrows, may reflect a critical attitude toward uninhibited behavior, with tendencies toward refinement and good grooming, perhaps overgrooming (Machover, 1949).
2. Bushy eyebrows suggest tendencies away from refinement and good grooming toward "primitive, gruff, and uninhibited" tendencies (Machover, 1949).
3. Raised eyebrows suggest an attitude of disdain (Machover, 1949).
4. Eyelashes detailed by males suggest possible homosexual tendencies (Machover, 1949).

Ear and Nose

A. *Large ears, strongly reinforced or viewed through transparent hair,* suggest:

1. Possible auditory handicap and associated concern (DiLeo, 1973; Machover, 1949).
2. Sensitivity to criticism (Buck, 1948; Jolles, 1964; Machover, 1949).

3. Possible ideas of reference (Burns & Kaufman, 1972; Machover, 1949).

B. *Nose emphasis through pressure or size* suggests:

1. Sexual difficulties and/or castration fears (Buck, 1948; Hammer, 1971; Jolles, 1964; Machover, 1949).
2. Feelings of sexual inadequacy or impotency, especially in older males (Machover, 1949).
3. With nostril indicated and emphasized, aggressive tendencies, and indication of association with psychosomatic asthmatic conditions (Burns & Kaufman, 1972; Machover, 1949).

Mouth and Chin

A. *Mouth emphasis* suggests:

1. Regressive defenses, orality (Burns & Kaufman, 1972; Jolles, 1964; Machover, 1949).
2. Oral emphasis in personality (DiLeo, 1973; Machover, 1949).
3. Primitive tendencies (Machover, 1949).
4. Possible speech problems (Machover, 1949).

B. *Mouth omitted* suggests:

1. Possible psychosomatic respiratory, asthmatic conditions (Machover, 1949).
2. Possible depressive conditions (Machover, 1949).
3. Reluctance to communicate with others (Buck, 1948).

C. *Miscellaneous treatment of mouth*:

1. Teeth showing, in adult drawings, suggests infantile, aggressive or sadistic tendencies (Buck, 1948; Burns & Kaufman, 1972; Machover, 1949).
2. Short heavy line for mouth suggests strong aggressive impulses, but anticipated retaliation makes the individual cautious (Machover, 1949).
3. Single-line mouths in profile suggest considerable tension (Machover, 1949).
4. Wide, upturned line effecting a grin is normal with children, but in adults suggests forced congeniality, and possibly inappropriate affect (Machover, 1949).

194

5. Cupid-bow mouth in female figures has been associated with sexually-precocious adolescent females and adult psychosomatic, asthmatic conditions (Machover, 1949).
6. Open mouths suggest oral passivity (Machover, 1949).
7. Objects in mouth such as cigarettes, toothpicks, pipes, etc. suggest oral erotic needs (Machover, 1949).

D. *Chin unusually emphasized* suggests:

1. Possible aggressive, dominant tendencies (Buck, 1948; Jolles, 1964; Machover, 1949).
2. Possible strong drive levels (Machover, 1949).
3. Possible compensation for feelings of weakness (Machover, 1949).

Neck and Adam's Apple

A. *General considerations*:

1. The neck, connecting link between head and body, has been regarded widely as the symbolic link between intellect and affect. Long necks are associated with dependency in the interpretation of human figure drawings. Most often, interpretive hypotheses regarding the neck are based on this rationale (Burns & Kaufman, 1972; Machover, 1949).

B. *Unusually short, thick necks* suggest:

1. Tendencies to be gruff, stubborn, "bull-headed" (Machover, 1949).
2. Impulse proclivities (Machover, 1949).

C. *Unusually long necks* suggest:

1. Cultured, socially stiff, even rigid, formal, overly moral persons (Machover, 1949).
2. Dependency (Burns & Kaufman, 1972).

Contact Features: Arms, Hands, Fingers, Legs, Feet

A. *Arms treated unusually*: Generally, the condition of the arms and their placement in the drawing reflect the condition and mode of a person's physical or manual contact with his environment.

195

1. Stiff arms at sides suggest a rigid, compulsive, inhibited personality (see also Stance Characteristics, p. 198) (Buck, 1948; Jolles, 1964; Machover, 1949).
2. Limp arms at sides suggest a generally ineffective personality (DiLeo, 1973; Machover, 1949).
3. Akimbo arms suggest well-developed narcissistic or "bossy" tendencies (Machover, 1949).
4. Mechanical, horizontal extension or arms at right angle to body suggest a simple, regressed individual with shallow, affectless contact with his environment (Machover, 1949).
5. Frail, flimsy, wasted, shrunken arms suggest physical or psychological weakness, feelings of inadequacy (Buck, 1948; Hammer, 1971; Jolles, 1964; Machover, 1949).
6. Reinforced arms, especially with emphasis on muscles, suggest power strivings, usually of a physical nature; when associated with broad shoulder, etc., have been linked with aggressive, assaultive tendencies (Burns & Kaufman, 1972; Jolles, 1964; Machover, 1949).
7. Long, strong arms suggest acquisitive and compensatory ambition, need for physical strength and active contact with the environment (Buck, 1948; Jolles, 1964; Machover, 1949).
8. Very short arms suggest lack of ambition, absence of striving with feelings of inadequacy (Buck, 1948; Burns & Kaufman, 1972; Jolles, 1964).
9. Omission of arms suggest guilt feelings, as with omitted hands, and extreme depression, general ineffectiveness, dissatisfaction with the environment and strong withdrawal tendencies (Machover, 1949).
10. Omission of arms in drawing the opposite sex suggests the person feels rejected by members of the opposite sex, perhaps by subject's opposite-sexed parent; occasionally reflects guilt feelings (Machover, 1947).
11. Omission of feet suggests feelings of instability or a lack of "roots" (Burns, 1982).

B. Hands

1. Vague or dim hands suggest a lack of confidence in social situations, or general lack of confidence or productivity, possibly both (Machover, 1949).

2. Shaded hands suggest anxiety and guilt feelings, usually associated with aggressive or masturbatory activity (Buck, 1948; Jolles, 1964; Machover, 1949).
3. Unusually large hands suggest aggressiveness (Burns & Kaufman, 1972).
4. Hands covering the genital region suggest autoerotic practices, and have been noted in drawings by sexually maladjusted females (Buck, 1948; Machover, 1949).
5. Swollen hands suggest inhibited impulses (Machover, 1949).
6. Omission of hands is of equivocal significance because they are the most frequently omitted feature of human drawings. However, this omission has been associated with feelings of inadequacy, castration fears, masturbatory guilt and organic conditions (Buck, 1948; Hammer, 1971).
7. Hands drawn last suggest feelings of inadequacy and a reluctance to make contact with the environment (Buck, 1948).
8. Fingers. The treatment of the fingers is often considered more important than the treatment of the hands or arms. Genetically, fingers are drawn before hands or arms. Fingers represent contact features in the strictest sense and obviously may be used in a wide variety of friendly, constructive, hostile and destructive ways.
9. Talon-like, dark, straight lines or spiked fingers suggest infantile, primitive, aggressive tendencies (Buck, 1948; Hammer, 1971; Jolles, 1964; Machover, 1949).
10. Clenched fists suggest aggression and rebelliousness (Buck, 1949; Machover, 1949).
11. Fingers without hands, common in children's drawings, suggest in adult drawings regression and infantile aggressive, assaultive tendencies, especially if in single dimension with heavy pressure (Machover, 1949).
12. Severely shaded or reinforced fingers generally have been regarded as indicative of guilt feelings and usually are associated with stealing or masturbation (Machover, 1949).
13. Unusually large fingers suggest aggressive, assaultive tendencies (Burns & Kaufman, 1972).

D. Legs

1. Very long legs suggest a strong need for autonomy (Buck, 1948; Jolles, 1964).

197

2. Refusal to draw legs, usually associated with refusal to draw the figure below the waist, or if only a very few sketchy lines are used, suggests an acute sexual disturbance or pathological constriction (Jolles, 1964; Machover, 1949).

E. *Feet*

1. Elongated feet have been associated with strong security needs and possible castration fears (Buck, 1948; Burns & Kaufman, 1972; Hammer, 1971; Jolles, 1964).
2. Small, especially tiny feet have been associated with insecurity, constriction, dependence and various psychosomatic conditions (Buck, 1948; Jolles, 1964; Machover, 1949).
3. Resistance to drawing feet suggests depressed tendencies, discouragement, frequently seen in drawings of physically withdrawn, including bedridden, patients (Machover, 1949).
4. Lack of feet is common in runaways (Burns & Kaufman, 1972).

Stance Characteristics

A. *Wide stance* suggests:

1. Aggressive defiance and/or insecurity (Buck, 1948; Jolles, 1964; Machover, 1949).
2. Especially when figure is in middle of page, aggressiveness, even assaultive aggressiveness, sometimes counteracted by insecurity and manifested by feet that are tiny, shaded, reinforced, or perhaps drawn by light pressure or the consistent use of ground lines (Machover, 1949).
3. When legs float into space and the whole figure slants, severe insecurity and dependency, as in chronic alcoholism (DiLeo, 1973; Machover, 1949).
4. When the line fades out with a drawing as described in interpretation 2 above, this may suggest hysteria, psychopathy or hysterical psychopathy (Machover, 1949).

Other Parts of Body (Trunk, Shoulders, Breasts, Waistline, Hips, Buttocks, Joints, Etc.)

A. *General considerations*: Characteristically, the body has been associated with basic drives. The development of drives and activity poten-

198

tials, growth and decline, and attitudes related to these conditions may be indicated by one's treatment of the trunk. Consequently, treatment of the trunk is more changeable with age. Frequently the trunk is drawn as a relatively simple, more or less rectangular to oval shape. Deviations from this must be considered unusual.

B. *Trunk treated unusually*:

1. Rounded trunks suggest a passive, less aggressive, relatively feminine, or perhaps infantile, regressive personality (Machover, 1949; Petersen, 1977).
2. Angular figures suggest a relatively masculine personality (Machover, 1949; Petersen, 1977).
3. Disproportionately small trunks suggest a denial of drives, feelings of inferiority, or both (Buck, 1948).
4. Reluctance to close bottom of trunk suggests sexual preoccupation (Machover, 1949).

C. *Shoulders treated unusually*: Generally, the treatment of shoulders is considered an expression of feelings of need for physical power.

1. Squared shoulders suggest aggressive, hostile tendencies (Buck, 1948; Hammer, 1971; Jolles, 1964).
2. Tiny shoulders suggest inferiority feelings (Buck, 1948; Jolles, 1964).
3. Erasure, reinforcement, or uncertainties in drawing shoulders suggest drive for body development; masculinity is a basic preoccupation. These signs are found in drawings of psychosomatic, hypertense patients (Machover, 1949).
4. In males, massive shoulders suggest aggressive tendencies or sexual ambivalence, often with a compensatory reaction, as in insecure individuals and adolescents (Hammer, 1971; Machover, 1949).

D. *Unusually large breasts drawn by males* suggest probable strong oral and dependency needs (Machover, 1949).

E. *Underclothed or nude figures* suggest:

1. Infantile, sexually maladjusting personalities, as with overclothing (Machover, 1949).

199

2. Voyeuristic tendencies (Machover, 1949).
3. Exhibitionistic tendencies (Machover, 1949).

F. *Clothes too big for figure* suggest feelings of inadequacy and self-disdain (Buck, 1948; Hammer, 1971).

G. *Transparent clothing* suggests voyeuristic and/or exhibitionistic tendencies (Machover, 1949).

H. *Button emphasis* suggests:

1. Dependent, infantile, inadequate personality (Burns & Kaufman, 1972; Jolles, 1964; Machover, 1949).
2. Regression, particularly when drawn mechanically down the middle (Buck, 1948; Jolles, 1964; Machover, 1949).
3. On cuffs, adds an obsessive tone to the dependency (Machover, 1949).

I. *Pocket emphasis* suggests:

1. Infantile, dependent male personality (Machover, 1949).
2. Affectional or maternal deprivation, which often contributes to psychopathic proclivities (Machover, 1949).
3. Large pockets emphasized, adolescent virility strivings with conflict involving emotional dependence on mother (Machover, 1949).

J. *Tie emphasis* suggests:

1. Feelings of sexual inadequacy, especially in adolescents and men over 40 years old (Buck, 1948; Jolles, 1964; Machover, 1949).
2. Tiny, uncertainly drawn, or debilitated ties suggest despairing awareness of weak sexuality (Machover, 1949).
3. Long and conspicuous ties suggest sexual aggressiveness, perhaps overcompensating for fear of impotence (Machover, 1949).

K. *Shoe emphasis* suggests:

1. Large shoe suggests need for stability (Burns & Kaufman, 1972).
2. With overdetailing of shoes, laces, etc., obsessive and distinctly feminine characteristics, most commonly observed in pubescent girls (Machover, 1949).

Miscellaneous Drawing Characteristics of Persons

A. *Body part "cut off" or occluded by another object* suggests:

1. Denial or repression of the occluded area and an inability to "think" about these areas (Burns & Kaufman, 1970).
2. With boys, fears of castration in competition with father, older brothers (Burns & Kaufman, 1970).
3. Found in significantly more drawings of emotionally disturbed vs. emotionally adjusted boys (Burns & Kaufman, 1972; Meyers, 1978).

B. *Cutting off the head* suggests concerns or dealings with issues of control (Burns & Kaufman, 1972).

C. *Crossing out and redrawing of an entire figure* suggests individual's true feelings or idealized feelings toward this person (or oneself, if drawing is of self) (Burns & Kaufman, 1970).

D. *Excessive erasure* suggests:

1. Uncertainty, indecisiveness, restlessness (Hammer, 1971; Machover, 1949).
2. Dissatisfaction with self (Hammer, 1971).
3. Possible anxiety (Machover, 1949).

E. *Inclusion of extra figures* suggests:

1. Disruptive influence protruding into the family (Reynolds, 1978).
2. Closeness within the extended family (Reynolds, 1978).

F. *Rotated figures* may indicate:

1. Feelings of disorientation (Burns & Kaufman, 1972).
2. Feelings of being different with respect to others (Burns & Kaufman, 1972).
3. Need for attention (Burns & Kaufman, 1972).
4. Association with feelings of rejection (Reynolds, 1978).
5. Neurological dysfunction (Reynolds, 1978).
6. Found more often in emotionally disturbed vs. emotionally adjusted boys (Burns & Kaufman, 1972; Meyers, 1978).

G. *Shading or crosshatching (scribbling or "blacking out" of a figure) or heavy shading (all except hair)*:

1. Found significantly more often in emotionally disturbed boys vs. emotionally adjusted boys (Burns & Kaufman, 1972; Meyers, 1978).
2. Found significantly less often in younger vs. older boys (Meyers, 1978).
3. Often-used style by middle-class adolescents (Thompson, 1975).

H. *Shading of specific body parts* suggests:

1. Preoccupation with the body part blackened (Burns & Kaufman, 1972).
2. Anxiety, perhaps about the body part blackened or issues around that body part (e.g., issues of sexuality when a body is blackened from the waist down) (Burns, 1982; Burns & Kaufman, 1970).

I. *General shading* indicates:

1. Possible depression (Burns & Kaufman, 1970).
2. Identification of significantly interacting individuals in a particular family dynamic (Burns, 1982; Burns & Kaufman, 1972).
3. Attempts to control or deny an impulse (Burns & Kaufman, 1972).

J. *Shading an individual or object* suggests preoccupation and/or anxiety with, inhibition towards or fixation on the person or object involved (Reynolds, 1978).

K. *Stick figures (where all figures are drawn as stick figures)* suggest:

1. Defensive or resistant reaction to the test setting, especially when whole drawings are completed upon request (Burns & Kaufman, 1972; Reynolds, 1978).
2. Low IQ (Reynolds, 1978).
3. Minimal cooperation, suggesting negativism (Hammer, 1971).

L. *Snow person* suggests emotional deprivation.

M. Transparencies indicate:

1. Showing parts of body through the clothing suggests voyeuristic tendencies in adults, though may be normal in children (Machover, 1949).
2. Organic problems (DiLeo, 1973).
3. Distortions of reality; poor, often tenuous reality testing (Reynolds, 1978).
4. For older children and adolescents possible psychosis, thought pattern disturbances (Reynolds, 1968).
5. Low IQ (Reynolds, 1978).

ADDITIONAL READINGS

Atkinson, A. J. John's Family in Kinetic Family Drawings. *The Commentary.* Vol. 1, No. 3, Bountiful, Utah: Carr Pub. Co., 1977.

Barker, P. *Using Metaphors in Psychotherapy.* New York: Brunner/Mazel, 1985.

Brewer, F. L. *Children's Interaction Patterns in Kinetic Family Drawings.* Dissertations Abstracts International, 41 4253B 1981.

Jacobson, D. A. *A Study of Kinetic Family Drawings of Public School Children Ages 6 through 9.* University of Cincinnati, 1974. Available through Dissertation Abstracts. Order #73-29-455.

Johnston, D. D. *Comparison of DAF and KFD in Children from Intact and Divorced Homes.* Thesis Abstracts. San Jose: California State Univ., 1975.

Kato, T. *Pictorial Expression of Family Relationships in Young Children.* IX International Congress of Psychopathology of Expression. Verona, Italy, 1979.

Kato, T., Ikura, H., Kubo, Y. A Study on the "Style" in Kinetic Family Drawing. *Japanese Bulletin of Art Therapy*, Vol. 7, 1976.

Kato, T., and Shimizu, T. The Action in KFD and the Child's Attitude Towards Family Members. *Japanese Bulletin of Art Therapy*, Vol. 9, 1978.

Kellogg, R. *Analyzing Children's Art.* California National Press Books, 1969.

Klepsch, M. and Logie L. *Children Draw and Tell.* New York: Brunner/Mazel, 1982.

Landgarten, H. B. *Clinical Art Therapy.* New York: Brunner/Mazel, 1982.

Lodesma, L. K. *The Kinetic Family Drawings of Filipino Adolescents.* Dissertation Abstracts International, 40 1866B 1979.

Mangum, M. E. *Familial Identification in Black, Anglo, and Chicano MR Children Using K-F-D.* Dissertation Abstracts International, 36 (11-A), 7343A 1976.

Mostkoff, D. L., and Lazarus, P. J. The Kinetic Family Drawing: The reliability of an objective scoring system. *Psychology in the Schools*, 20, 16-20, 1983.

Rama, S., Ballentine, R., and Ajaya, S. *Yoga and Psychotherapy*. Illinois: Himalayan Institute, 1976.

Raskin, L. M. and Bloom, A. S. Kinetic Family Drawings by Children with Learning Disabilities. *Journal of Pediatric Psychology*, 4, 247-251, 1979.

Raskin, L. M. and Pitcher, G. B. Kinetic Family Drawings by Children with Perceptual-Motor Delays. *Journal of Learning Disabilities*, 10, 370-374, 1977.

Reynolds, D. K. *The Quiet Therapies. Japanese Pathways to Personal Growth*. University Press of Hawaii, 1980.

Rhine, P. C. *Adjustment Indicators in Kinetic Family Drawings by Children: A Validation Study*. Dissertation Abstracts International. 39. (2-8). 995. 1978.

Roth, J. and Huber, G. *Familiendynamik, Sonderdruck, aus Jahrgang*. Stuttgart: Klett-Cotta, 1979.

Sayed, A. J. and Leaverton, D. R. Kinetic Family Drawings of Children with Diabetes. *Child Psychiatry and Human Development*, 5, 40-50, 1974.

Schornstein, H. H. and Derr, J. The Many Applications of Kinetic Family Drawings in Child Abuse. *British Journal of Projective Psychology and Personality Study*, 23, 33-35, 1978.

Souza de Joode, M. O Desenho Cinetico da Familia (KFD) coma Instrumento de Deagnostico da Dinamica do Relacinonamento Familiar. *Auquivos Brasileiros de Psicologia Aplicada*: 29 (2), 149-162, Abr/Jun 1976. Rio de Janeiro, Brazil.

Straus, M. A. *Family Measurement Techniques*. University of Minn. Press, 1977.

REFERENCES

ALSCHULER, R. H. and HATTWICK, L. W. *Painting and Personality. A Study of Young Children (Vol. 2)*. Chicago: University of Chicago Press, 1947.

BUCK, J. N. The H-T-P technique: A qualitative and quantitative scoring manual. *J. Clin. Psychol.*, 4, 397–405, 1978.

BUCK, J. W. and HAMMER, E. F. (Eds.) *Advances in House-Tree-Person Techniques: Variations and Applications*. Los Angeles: Western Psychological Services, 1969.

BURNS, R. C. *Kinetic Family Drawings: Practice and Research Panel*. Annual Meeting of the American Association of Psychiatric Services for Children. November, 1979, Chicago. Taperecording. Audio Transcripts Ltd., New York, N.Y.

BURNS, R. C. What children are telling us in their human figure drawings. *Early Childhood Educ. Council*. Vol. 11. No. 3. Saskatoon, Saskatchewan, Canada, 1980.

BURNS, R. C. *Self-Growth in Families: Kinetic Family Drawing (K-F-D) Research and Application*. New York: Brunner/Mazel, 1982.

BURNS, R. C. and KAUFMAN, S. H. *Kinetic Family Drawings (K-F-D): An Introduction to Understanding Children Through Kinetic Drawings*. New York: Brunner/Mazel, 1970.

BURNS, R. C. and KAUFMAN, S. H. *Actions, Styles and Symbols in Kinetic Family Drawings (K-F-D): An Interpretative Manual*. New York: Brunner/Mazel, 1972.

BURNS, R. C. and REPS, P. Women: To need or to love? *The Tarrytown Letter*, No. 52. October, 1985.

CHIANG, H. M. and MASLOW, A. H. *The Healthy Personality: Readings*. New York: Van Nostrand, 1969.

COWARD, H. Jung and Eastern Thought. New York: State University of New York Press, 1985.

DiLEO, J. H. *Children's Drawings as Diagnostic Aids*. New York: Brunner/Mazel, 1973.

FRANK, F. *The Zen of Seeing*. New York: Vintage Books, Random House, 1973.

GOODENOUGH, F. L. *Measurement of Intelligence by Drawings*. New York: Harcourt, Brace and World, Inc., 1926.

HAMMER, E. F. Hierarchical organization of personality and the H-T-P, achromatic and chromatic. In Buck J. N. and Hammer, E. F. (Eds.) *Advances in House-Tree-Person Techniques: Variations and Applications*. Los Angeles: Western Psychological Services, 1969, pp. 1–35.

HAMMER, E. F. *The Clinical Application of Projective Drawings*. Springfield, IL: Charles C Thomas, 1971.

HARRIS, D. B. *Children's Drawings as Measures of Intellectual Maturity*. New York: Harcourt, Brace and World, 1963.

HEINEMAN, T. *Kinetic Family Drawings of Siblings of Severely Emotionally Disturbed Children*. Thesis Abstracts. School of Social Welfare, University of California at Berkeley, 1975.

HULSE, W. C. The emotionally disturbed child draws his family. *Quart J. Child Behavior*, 3, 152–174, 1951.

JOLLES, I. *A Catalogue for the Qualitative Interpretation of the House-Tree-Person (H-T-P)*. Los Angeles: Western Psychological Services, 1964.

JUNG, C. G. *The Portable Jung*. New York: Pegasus Books, 1976.

JUNG, C. G. *Word and Image*. Bollingen Series XCVII, Princeton, NJ: Princeton University Press, 1979.

KLEPSCH, M. and LOGIE, L. *Children Draw and Tell*. New York: Brunner/Mazel, 1982.

KNOFF, H. M. Justifying projective/personality assessment in school psychology: A response to Batsche and Peterson. *School Psychology Review*, 12, 446–451, 1983a.

KNOFF, H. M. Personality assessment in the schools: Issues and procedures for school psychologists. *School Psychology Review*, 12, 224–232, 1983b.

KNOFF, H. M. and PROUT, H. T. *Kinetic Drawing System for Family and School: A Handbook*. Los Angeles: Western Psychological Services, 1985.

KOPPITZ, E. M. *Psychological Evaluation of Children's Human Figure Drawing*. New York: Grune and Stratton, 1968.

MACHOVER, K. *Personality Projection in the Drawing of the Human Figure*. Springfield, IL: Charles C Thomas, 1949.

MASLOW, A. H. *Motivation and Personality*. New York: Harper and Row, 1954.

MASLOW, A. H. *Toward a Psychology of Being*. New York: Van Nostrand, 1962.

MASLOW, A. H. *Religions, Values, and Peak-Experiences*. Columbus: Ohio State University, 1964.

MASLOW, A. H. Criteria for judging needs to be instinctoid. In M. R. Jones (ed.), *Human Motivation: A Symposium*. Lincoln: University of Nebraska Press. 1965.

METZNER, R. The tree as a symbol of self unfoldment. *The American Theosophist*, Fall, 1981.

MEYERS, D. Toward an objective evaluation procedure for the Kinetic Family Drawings (K-F-D). *Journal of Personality Assessment*, 42, 358–365, 1978.

O'BRIEN, R. O. and PATTON, W. F. Development of an objective scoring method for the Kinetic Family Drawing. *Journal of Personality Assessment*, 38, 156–164, 1974.

PETERSEN, C. S. Roots as shown in Kinetic Family Drawings. *The Commentary*, 1(3), 1–6, 1977. Bountiful, UT: Carr Publishing Co.

PROUT, H. T. and CELMER, D. S. School drawings and academic achievement: A validity study of the Kinetic School Drawing Technique. *Psychology in the Schools*, 21, 176–180, 1984.

PROUT, H. T. and PHILLIPS, P. D. A clinical note: The Kinetic School Drawing. *Psychology in the Schools*, 11, 303–306, 1974.

REYNOLDS, C. R. A quick-scoring guide to the interpretation of children's Kinetic Family Drawings (K-F-D). *Psychology in the Schools*, 15, 489–492, 1978.

SARBAUGH, M. E. *Kinetic Drawing-School (Kd-S) Technique*. Illinois School Psychologists' Association Monograph Series, 1, 1–70, 1982.

THOMPSON, P. L. *Kinetic Family Drawings of Adolescents*. Dissertation Abstracts. California School of Professional Psychology, San Francisco, 1975.

WOHL, A., and KAUFMAN, B. *Silent Screams and Hidden Cries*. New York: Brunner/Mazel, 1985.

WOLFF, W. *The Personality of the Pre-School Child*. New York: Grune and Stratton, 1946.

INDEX

211